"OFFLINE presents an insightful and convincing argument for the need for humans and societies to protect the most valuable resource of our time: attention."

Jens Hjorth-Larsen, Consultant, 29 years, no kids.

"Crazy that it's only when you change your bad habits and lifestyle that you realize how little you lived life before."

Mette Stryhn, CEO and Mother of three.

"An amazing, easily understandable book, providing both a significant eyeopener for your own behavior and a tangible help for a healthier digital life."

Kim Sylvestersen, Section Manager, Father of one.

"What an eyeopener! Taught me how to get a healthier relationship with my smartphone."

Anders Røpke, Wind Power Lab CEO and Father of two.

"If your children use smartphones, you need to read this book!"

Teresa Egballe, Municipal Manager and Mother of three

"Required reading for any parent with smartphone-kids."

Søren H. Mohr, CEO, Father of two.

"Is your phone in control of your life? Read this book and find out!"

Niklas Laugesen, CEO at Napp.

"Made a huge impact on me and I'm grateful that I got the message."

Lotte Thor Høgsbjerg, Founder SPIB media, Mother of two.

"Wow! I had no idea about how powerful these brain-hacks are. Must read!"

Tone Folkedal, GP, Mother of two.

"What a well written wake-up-call! Now I understand why it has been so hard to get away from my smartphone. Thanks!"

— Sarah Thorngreen Auken, Mother of two and parish priest.

"Shows you how to get the most out of being online without being sucked into wasting your time. Great for families with kids."
Maria von Würden, Registered nurse, Mother of two.

"My two kids change their behavior if they spend too much time online. Now I understand why and have set easy to follow rules for how and when they are online"
Charlotte Just Nielsen, Selfemployed and Mother of two.

"Wow. What a wake up call. Today I recommended this book to my patients and have become much more aware of how my own family uses smartphones and ipads."
Michael Hejmadi, MD, GP and Father of two.

"Canned social recognition. What a sharp insight. This book is a must-read! Our public sector and kids need to be made more aware!"
Mette Ernlund, PhD and Mother of two.

"Loved the book and the theories – almost felt guilty reading as an ebook on my smartphone . . . ."
Jens Balle, Sales Rep. and Father of three.

"Learn how to get the online world to work for you without being tricked and trapped into its addictive design. Recommended reading."
Amira Saric, CSR-specialist and Mother of three.

"Thought provoking. Made me put my phone away and start prioritizing what's important for me and my family".
Kasper Mortensen, Prepress Technician and Father of three.

COMHAIRLE CHONTAE ÁTHA CLIATH THEAS
SOUTH DUBLIN COUNTY LIBRARIES

BALLYROAN BRANCH LIBRARY
TO RENEW ANY ITEM TEL: 494 1900
OR ONLINE AT www.southdublinlibraries.ie

Items should be returned on or before the last date below. Fines, as displayed in the Library, will be charged on overdue items.

4/10/19		

This edition first published 2019
© 2019 Imran Rashid and Gerald Soren Kenner

Registered office
John Wiley & Sons Ltd, The Atrium, Southern Gate, Chichester, West Sussex, PO19
8SQ, United Kingdom

For details of our global editorial offices, for customer services and for information about
how to apply for permission to reuse the copyright material in this book please see our
website at www.wiley.com.

Library of Congress Cataloging-in-Publication Data is available.

ISBN 978-0-857-08793-5 (paperback)
ISBN 978-0-857-08794-2 (ePDF)
ISBN 978-0-857-08792-8 (ePub)

10 9 8 7 6 5 4 3 2 1

Cover Design: Wiley
Brain Image: © Denis Maliugin/Shutterstock,
Cord Image: © CW craftsman/Shutterstock

Set in 12/16pt AGaramondPro by SPi Global, Chennai, India
Printed in Great Britain by TJ International Ltd, Padstow, Cornwall, UK

Imran: Thanks to my two kids Sarah and Isak for letting me witness the miracle of two incredible, fantastic human beings growing up. Every single day with you guys is a gift. And also a big thank you to my wife Naomi. Without you, I wouldn't be me.

Soren: Thank you to my wonderful Helen, Sarah, and Thomas for patience and encouragement, for putting up with my being distracted and for the many good discussions around the dinner table (even if I do have to Messenger you all to get anyone to show up).

CONTENTS

ACKNOWLEDGMENTS

This book could not have been written without input from experts in many different fields. In particular we would like to thank Professor of Neurobiology Albert Gjedde (Center of Neuroscience at Copenhagen University); Jacob Geday, MD (neurologist and neuroscience researcher); Anette Prehn, MD (sociologist and science communicator), and Kristian Moltke Martiny, PhD (post-doc at the Center for Subjectivity Research, Copenhagen University) for taking time to review and critique our work. Thank you to Martin Booe for outstanding editorial consultancy, to Sarah Kenner for editing input and pointing out Ben Okri, and to Karen Weller for quick and pinpoint accurate copy-editing. You have made this a better book than it otherwise would have been. It goes without saying that any remaining errors and flaws are ours.

Introduction: Offline

I f this book caught your attention, then you're already
concerned about the effect digital devices are having on your
life. You've read about younger people who have thousands of
friends on Facebook but no real-life social skills. You've got a
good sense that distraction is not good and that you can waste
a lot of time reacting to notifications, unnecessary texts, and
selfies your cousin blasts you from Ibiza. You can now order
your coffee with an app, thus saving you at least 45 seconds
of interaction with a human intermediary. But what have we
really gained?

You don't have to be a psychologist to see that smartphones
and tablets are changing the way we act and interact with each
other, and not necessarily in a good way. But have you considered that smartphones are even changing the way we *walk*?
Think about this: if you compare footage of people walking
down a street 20 years ago with what you see today, you'll see
that the human gait has changed. Twenty years ago, people
walked with their heads mostly up and their eyes focused on
the territory before them, scanning side to side for potential
dangers, or possibly friends, and not uncommonly a potential
romantic partner. (This quaint folk practice was commonly
known as "watching where you're going"!) Today, the head
is down, the shoulders are forward, the spine folds inward

and the lower back juts out. All of these postural adjustments are brought to us by the smartphone we're holding out in front of us as if it were a recently added body part. The funky smartphone dance is already an orthopedical disaster that will soon be felt in the neck and pelvis, but that's not half of it.

First, it hardly needs to be said that a city walk with your eyes glued to your smartphone boosts your chances of getting run over by a car or a truck. That's because your physical environment now is of only *secondary* concern because your attention is on your device. It's not all that different from walking through a jungle and not paying attention to tigers, or not paying any attention to your tribal members warning you about tigers because you're totally fixated on something that has nothing to do with your immediate environment.

So, to conserve energy, the brain shifts into a primal scan mode that alerts it only to the threat of physical danger—but not even doing that very well. But that's *still* not even half of it.

Do you feel the chill at your local cafe, where the friendly banter has been replaced by gloomy silence? Meanwhile, the room is jittery with the flash of dozens of small, bright electronic screens. Almost everyone is entirely absorbed by their smartphone or tablet navigating their own private online bubble. At the playground, parents on benches are staring into smartphones while their kids unsuccessfully try to get their attention. Even at restaurants or dinner at home it is not uncommon to see friends and families all glued to their smartphones.

Yes, smartphones and social media deliver a lot of goods, literally and figuratively. But it's also becoming clearer day by day that our digital fixation is depleting our nervous systems individually and collectively. Digital devices have cast a chill over human relationships and interactions that we are only just starting to recognize, let alone understand or counteract. Maybe now is the time for a digital counter-revolution?

Our global adoption of digital technology happened in an extraordinarily short span of time, such that it has summarily outpaced our ability to absorb it on a cultural level as well as a neurological one. Maybe it's time to unplug from the matrix for a while and assess the damage wrought as well as the benefits brought to us by our new digital lifestyle.

We initially decided to write this book because we felt trapped by smartphones constantly clamoring for our attention and constantly pulling us away from what was happening here and now in the real world. But as we probed deeper into the research and observed what was happening around us, we came to understand that the problem extends profoundly beyond time management issues.

That discussion sparked a book in Danish titled SLUK (meaning, "Turn It Off!") about the effects of being constantly connected and online. The book was on the national bestseller list for 18 months. It sparked a heated debate in Denmark and has led to the establishment of a government panel on stress and digital habits and the decision to fund more research into the area.

What started out as SLUK eventually became this book, *Offline*, that presents a much deeper look into digital behavior and its consequences. As we began sifting through an ever-growing body of research that connects smartphones and social media with stress, sleep disturbances, concentration issues, decision fatigue, escapism, cognitive bias and so on, we came to realize four things:

1. The sheer size of the industry servicing us with smartphones, social media, games, news, and so on. Companies like Apple, Google, Facebook and Amazon are essentially empires with economies that rival those of many countries.

2. That in the twenty-first century, the power of *attention* has become an incredibly important commodity because in essence it fuels all online shopping. The longer these companies can keep your eyeballs glued to the screen looking at their product, the more money they make. This may be good business but may be not so good for you.

3. That extended and uncontrolled use of smartphones, social media, online gaming and the like have serious consequences in terms of your ability to focus, concentrate, learn, connect and be in the real world.

4. That a significant cause of these issues is the consistent use of "brain hacks," also known as addictive design, in the technology you use. These "hacks" are designed to install "triggers" that you are not consciously aware of, but which create an urge to be online, to check notifications and mail, or to scroll endlessly through social media newsfeeds.

All leading to a syndrome we have named DFRAG (digital fragmentation syndrome). This term describes a condition where the human experience of time, space and consciousness is constantly fragmented through digital interactions. When humans constantly lose sight of who they are, where they are and what their conscious goal is, we believe this leads to serious biological, psychological and social symptoms. DFRAG is what happens when you start using technology because you want to, but end up using it because you can't resist doing so because a number of triggers have been installed into the more automated thought and behavior patterns in your brain and are now making it difficult for you to function at optimal levels—making it hard to be at your best, whether in terms of family life, your work or your leisure time.

And yes—this is something that we will document as you read on!

Are You Being Digitally Manipulated?

It is hard, if not impossible, to imagine life without the Internet, but perhaps even harder to fathom how very suddenly and very recently this all happened. Amazon was founded in 1994, Google in 1998, Facebook in 2004, YouTube in 2005, Twitter in 2006 and Instagram in 2010.

Today these companies are fixtures in our world and through them everything seems to be just a click or two away. A human being with an internet connection and a credit card can have practically anything delivered with the click of a mouse. There is more to do, more to choose from and many more ways of sharing than ever before.

By 2019 more than 5 billion people will have smartphones and there will be around 1.5 billion tablets in the world. We will be just short of 8 billion people on the planet and almost half of us—3.7 billion—will have internet access. More than one-third of the world's population will be using one or more social networks to keep in touch with friends, exchange ideas, watch videos, play games, take quizzes, join groups, collect likes and post photos.

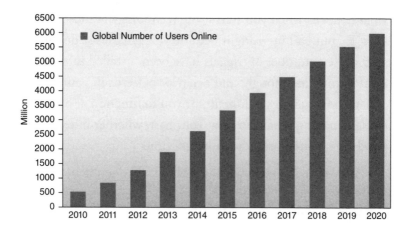

Soon there will be 6 billion smartphone users in the world. That's pretty much 75% of the total global population.

A funny thing didn't happen on the way to Digital Oz, though. Until recently, nobody really stopped to ask what the mental, physical and social effects of all of this online activity would be. The mere existence of these platforms has been earth-shaking—that much was apparent from the beginning.

However, nobody particularly wanted to ask an uncomfortable question: What happens to your mind when digital marketers start manipulating your brain chemistry through digital devices, which you carry around at all times, always available and always turned on?

It is amazing how unquestioning most of us are with regard to our relationship with our devices.

Think about it for a second: Is your smartphone the first thing you see in the morning and the last thing you see before sleeping? Have you become easier to distract over the past couple of years? Has it become harder to read longer texts than it used to be? Do you check your mail or social media while watching TV or even when driving your car? Do you feel the urge to repeatedly check your phone, even when you know that nothing new has arrived? Have you ever felt vibrations from your pocket and whipped out your phone just to discover that it was just your mind playing tricks on you (a phenomenon known as phantom pocket vibrations[1])?

Every one of these symptoms and many more are the clear consequences of the already mentioned DFRAG syndrome—the scary side effect of the digital manipulation strategies being used against you by large tech companies. Hundreds of millions of people are experiencing this new form of digital pollution and its effects can be just as toxic to the body and mind as contaminants elsewhere in the environment.

In short, your smartphone has become a platform for advanced "mind hacks" designed to capture and keep your attention fixed in order to resell it to advertisers, using a set of approaches collectively known as "addictive design." The battleground: smartphones, tablets, and laptops. The armies: providers of attention-seeking social media, games, search and other online services. The casualties: basically, every single important human activity worth paying attention to or spending time on, such as close relations, work, parenting, recreational activities, reading or sleep.

Access to Your Attention Has Become a Commodity

You may not be shocked to learn that there's a lot of money at stake in this quest to commodify attention. In 2017, advertisers paid more than $200 billion to gain access to your attention (Google got $109 billion of that and Facebook $40 billion). During the same period, consumers spent almost $500 billion buying smartphones, tablets and laptops.

What happens in an internet minute?

Source: Visual Capitalist/Business Insider.

Addictive design may just be the natural progress of smart business, but in regard to our digital devices, the old phrase *caveat emptor*—"let the buyer beware"—was never more relevant. When it comes to addictive design, no one is going to level the playing field between marketer and device owner, but each of us individually. That's why it's important to be able to identify addictive design before an app or platform gets its hooks into your brain stem—which, as you will see, it literally does. The "what happens in an internet minute"-graph shows you that the amount of information aimed at human eyeballs at any given moment is almost inconceivable. Remember, not a single piece of information originates in the digital world without eventually being processed, analyzed and responded to by human beings. Meaning that the actual fuel used to drive the digital transformation in our modern world is in fact our limited mental resources.

Once you understand how addictive design works and what it does to you, you will have no trouble identifying it on your smartphone, tablet or laptop. It comes in many disguises: notifications, emojis, cliffhangers, pickups, forever-scrolls, fear-of-missing-out and other effects. All of these are designed to spark your curiosity and to start up a shooting match with your dopamine triggers and set off a new cycle of craving–action–reward. This effect, often known as "stickiness," is of obvious value to the companies that vie to capture and resell your attention—but as it turns out it also causes stress, tampers with your attention span, reduces your ability to concentrate and focus and leads to a distorted view of the world—and maybe even yourself!

Technology Is Good. But Use it Carefully!

Technology is always a double-edged sword. Conscious use of it toward a positive and focused goal can do enormous good, while continuous idle use is probably not going to lead anywhere good.

On a global scale, technological advances, competition, free markets and increased trade have altogether provided and continue to provide incredible benefits—the world as we know it today is richer than ever before. It has less poverty, less hunger, less illness, less violence (truly—despite the impression the media may have given you) and delivers a better quality of life, more hope, more education and more democracy than ever before.[2]

Most people realize that spending your life on the couch eating junk food, smoking cigarettes and drinking gallons of alcohol will shorten your life[3] while eating a healthy diet and exercising regularly bestows a longer life span. But did you know that you boost your longevity even more by having close relationships with friends, family, partners or even pets?[4] And shouldn't this fact alone make us take a closer look at the extent to which the lightning quick near-universal adoption of digital devices in developed countries poses a threat to our ability to form close relationships and bond with other humans in real life?

Few, if any, foresaw the emergence of the massive "digital pollution" we all face today as a result of an almost exponential growth in the tech industry driven by commercial incentives to distract as many people as much as possible for as long as possible, or the resulting DFRAG-syndrome. DFRAG is a term we've coined to describe the contamination of our psycho-social environments and cognitive abilities and while the dangers of digital pollution may not yet be recognized by the general public to the same extent as other unhealthy lifestyle choices, research into the area over the last 10 years has been extensive, and there is no doubt that the potential detrimental effects are significant and grave.

In fact, we in no way feel like we're going out on a limb by calling this a "syndrome"—DFRAG (digital fragmentation syndrome) does indeed have a specific and demonstrable effect on your power of attention, your ability to concentrate and your ability to make conscious choices.

Here are some of the most common DFRAG symptoms resulting from extended exposure to digital pollution:

Physiologically

- Sleep disturbances. Poorer sleep quality and less of it.
- "Skin hunger" leading to psychological symptoms by lack of touches or hugs by others.
- Neural rewiring. Changes in how your brain works over time, a particular concern for children.
- Increased stress levels. Significant increase in physical stress levels.
- Reduced ability to recover from stress measurable in the body's level of stress hormones.
- Less physical activity due to screen time.
- Less sex and intimate relations.

Psychologically

- Reduced mental agility. Decision fatigue and mental overload.

- Diminished impulse control. Increased level of impulsive behavior.

- Problems making decisions. Increased number of "automated responses."

- Diminished attention span. Problems maintaining focus.

- Increasingly reactive behavior. Less proactive behavior.

- Reduced creativity and imagination.

- Decreased self-confidence. Feeling less in control.

- Lower self-esteem. Makes you feel your life isn't interesting enough.

Socially

- Diminished empathy. Becoming less able to empathize with others.

- Reduced social interaction. Moving from the "real world" into the online sphere.

- Increased polarization. Increased participation in negative "tribal" behavior.

- Increased feelings of loneliness. Fear of being left out.

- Increase in antisocial traits. Diminishing of societal coherence.

- Reality distortion. Cognitive dissonance. Echo-chamber effects.

As you will come to realize, these disturbing symptoms of digital pollution are not caused by some "evil big business conspiracy" nor are there any "mad geniuses" out there purposefully making designs that stress you out. What is happening is in some ways worse. It is the unintended and unpredicted consequence of the meeting between a fragile human cognitive sensorium developed by three million years of evolution consisting of an ongoing adaptation by the brain to the physical and mental environment and more than 60 000 years of socialization with a new technology that uses Big Data and constant optimization by algorithms to globally co-opt, influence and modify a large number of the basic thought and behavior patterns that our behavior, our identity and our culture are based on!

Digital pollution is insidious and not always perceptible. The fact that it came upon us practically in one fell swoop overnight means we adapted our behavior to it, rather than adapting the device to our actual needs. The other thing we didn't know was that the device reciprocates our embrace of it by "rewiring" our brains to suit its own purposes. This is not exactly what most people would consider a fair trade-off. Especially so in light of the fact that we have no idea what the long-term consequences are of this rewiring.

We will document that this impact of pervasive smart technology in our society is invasive and potentially dangerous.

The point of this book, however, is not to usher in a new age of technological Luddism, nor argue that technology is inherently bad. Rather, we want to deliver a nuanced and research-based understanding of the effects of digital pollution that will support a more conscious relationship to a device that has enormous transformative power—in both positive and negative ways, depending on the user and the usage.

We aim to help oppose addictive behavioral patterns that may be set off by a relentless bombardment of signals vying for your attention. We believe there's a way to enjoy the benefits of digital devices and platforms while protecting ourselves against the literal brain damage that can be caused by injudicious use. However, we are also quite confident that the phrase DFRAG, or "Digital Fragmentation Syndrome," will become common parlance in the coming years. When you start taking note of all the situations where technology makes people snap out of time, space or conscious behavior, you'll find yourself asking the same questions: Are we living in a world, where humans use technology to become better humans—or in a world where tech firms are exploiting humans just to form larger corporations?

Fortunately, this development and the damage caused by it is reversible, and in this book, we will show you how.

The authors of this book come from quite different backgrounds. Imran is a family doctor accustomed to dealing with human physiology and psychology. Soren is an advertising executive with a deep understanding of persuasive marketing and social media design. We also are both entrepreneurs with considerable experience from building businesses that include online advertising agencies, medical consultations by video, online share trading and even a subscription service that helps parents further the creative skills of their children. We believe these experiences and different backgrounds, combined with analysis of current research, gives us a unique insight into the opportunities, challenges and predicaments that this strange new universe presents.

The Internet, like every other significant technology, is a double-edged sword. On one hand, it's the solution to a number of major challenges we are facing as individuals and as societies. On the other hand, it's the harbinger of new challenges and threats. The best path forward lies in regaining mastery of the device that has attained mastery over us. Technology should be human-centric, and this human-centric viewpoint should be used to gauge the benefits and dangers of new technologies.

How This Book Is Structured

We want to give you the full picture—what the tech industry is doing, how it impacts your brain and what you can do to get rid of unwanted digital habits.

To do that, we start out with an overview of the tech industry to give you an idea of its size and scope. From there we take you on a discovery tour of the brain and the evolution of consciousness (important to know in order to understand how "mind hacks" work).

The next stop is taking a closer look at the "digital fix" and the use of "mind hacks," plus a closer look at the unintended side effects.

And finally, in the last part of the book we will show you a number of different techniques to tear down unwanted digital habits and replace them with patterns that work for you.

The point we are making is not that technology (especially smartphones, tablets, laptops and social media of all sorts) is bad but simply that when used in a wrong way it has consequences you should be aware of so you can make your own decision on what comprises sensible use for you.

Enjoy!

Notes

1. https://www.psychologytoday.com/us/blog/rewired-the-psychology-technology/201305/phantom-pocket-vibration-syndrome

2. https://singularityhub.com/2017/10/12/why-the-world-is-still-better-than-you-think-new-evidence-for-abundance/#sm.0001xzu47caaxf ciwe72q98f0ver1

3. Although still longer than the average lifespan was in the US just 100 years ago: 36 years for men and 42 years for women.

4. https://news.harvard.edu/gazette/story/2017/04/over-nearly-80-years-harvard-study-has-been-showing-how-to-live-a-healthy-and-happy-life/

Chapter One

A Tsunami of Technological Transformation

The Internet and its complementary technologies—particularly smartphones and tablets—have been the biggest cultural tsunami to hit the world since the steam engine brought about the industrial revolution in the mid-nineteenth century. Billions of people are now connected to each other, as well as to a seemingly inexhaustible supply of gossip, entertainment, news, music, films, TV and more. In a scant 25 years, we've gone from a world in which few had heard of emails to one in which even people living in the barest of shanties are wired in. And in the time, it probably took you to read the last paragraph, eight million emails and two million messages were opened, 300 000 posts were liked on Facebook and 100 000 Snaps, 50 000 tweets and 10 000 Instagram posts were created!

IBM estimates that 90 percent of all "information" ever created by humans, starting with the first cave paintings, has been produced within the past two years![1] According to Eric Schmidt, former CEO of Google, humans now create as much information every two days as they did during the entire span of time between the dawn of civilization through 2003—something like five exabytes of data every 48 hours.[2] And this is just the beginning.

New technologies are emerging at a frenetic pace—artificial intelligence, robotics, automation, blockchains and digital currencies will soon be added to the mix of new trends that already include online shopping, the streaming of film, TV and movies, social media, electronic banking, online dating, and much more. All of it is easily accessible by pretty much anyone from pretty much anywhere by smartphone or tablet. We are in the middle of an incredible transformation. A new age of connectedness that empowers individuals and breaks down barriers to make life easier, richer and fuller of possibility than ever before.

The speed with which we engage in this transformation is simply staggering: "By 2020, the number of smartphones, tablets and PCs in use will reach about 7.3 billion units," according to Peter Middleton, research director at Gartner.[3] What's really mind-blowing is that so few people seem surprised to learn that, practically in the blink of an eye, seemingly every man, woman and child on the planet will possess perhaps the most disruptive technology ever created in the form of a smartphone or a tablet.

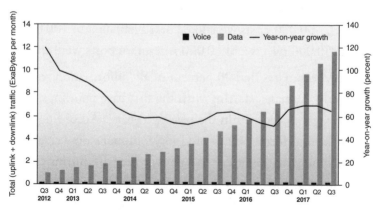

Reproduced with permission. Redrawn from Ericsson Mobility Report June 2018.[4]

Of course, the word "phone" is a misnomer when joined with the word "smart," because these devices are being used less and less as phones and more and more as hand-held computers. The graph from Ericsson on page 18 illustrates the staggering surge in data access through smartphones over a five-year period beginning in 2012.

Imperceptible Change

While the move toward digital connectivity may be the most massive tectonic shift in human history, most of us are scarcely aware of how deeply it is affecting us at the biological and psychological level. You've probably heard the story of how a frog immersed in cold water that is heated up gradually will allow itself to be boiled alive rather than jump out of the pot. That's because the change in temperature occurs too slowly for the frog's primitive nervous system to notice. You might say that the same is happening to our brains, individually and collectively, and the true impact of digital interaction on our lives—despite being overwhelming—is going largely unnoticed.

Today, information is always at your fingertips: you can now find anything from the operating hours of your local cafe to a list of the Best Horror Movies of 1982 in a matter of seconds. On YouTube you can listen to just about any song ever recorded. You can have your extra-hot soy chai latte waiting for you at the counter at Starbucks when you arrive, thanks to the many apps that are transforming the service industry (and many other industries as well). But this ability to project our wishes across the time–space continuum through digital technology comes with a price, and it's one that we are only now beginning to understand.

Think about the energy that just a visit to your favorite coffee shop demands of your nervous system. The number of choices is astonishing and choosing requires far more energy than you might realize. You might think that ordering coffee with an app is pretty cushy compared to being a hunter-gatherer who, whilst out in the forest, finds himself preyed upon by a tiger. One could argue quite handily, however, that the occasional dose of primal jeopardy (being chased by a tiger) has a way of keeping humans grounded or more focused. The importance of being able to become fully immersed in activities that require your full attention and are highly purpose-filled (such as hunting) is something we will return to in later chapters.

What is almost as amazing as all this new technology is how quickly we've come to take connectivity for granted. And yet, the technology we have now will no doubt seem laughably primitive in a few more years, when it's entirely possible that smartphones will be replaced by intelligent glasses or even devices embedded under your skin, making a search for information as simple as thinking about it. As a matter of fact many researchers are already working on direct brain-to-internet connectivity[5] and the first practical applications have already been developed: prosthetics for lost arms or legs that operate by the power of thought! At the World Government Summit in 2017,[6] Tesla and Space-X founder Elon Musk said:

> Humans must become cyborgs if they are to stay relevant in a future dominated by artificial intelligence … There will be fewer and fewer jobs that a robot can't do better. If humans want to continue to add value to the economy, they must augment their capabilities through a merger of biological intelligence and machine intelligence. If we fail to

do this, we'll risk becoming "house cats" to artificial intelligence.

A controversial viewpoint, but still an indication of how uncertain the future is and the level of impact some think technology will have on it. The transformation is already well underway, and the road ahead shows no sign of slowing growth—quite the reverse in fact. The near-exponential growth we have witnessed with the advent of the Internet seems set to continue for quite some time to come.

Because Your Eyeballs Are Worth It

Why would anybody want to brain-hack nice people like us? You may not be entirely surprised to learn that doing so is BIG BUSINESS. So, before we get to the "how" they do it, let's pause to consider *who* is doing this to us and *why*.

When you pick up a smartphone or tablet and interact with the web, you're not just connecting to a ubiquitous and rapidly growing layer of information: you are tapping into an infrastructure designed and managed by a new breed of behemoths. Although these companies are usually only ten or twenty years old, many have revenues that are larger than the economy of countries like Sweden, Italy or the Netherlands.

The reason companies like Apple and Amazon are currently valued at around a trillion dollars each is, in essence, because there's a lot of money to be made selling smartphones and providing access to online services—around $500 billion a year (or a stack of hundred-dollar bills about 500 kilometers tall!).

Incidentally, that's just about the size of the annual Swedish Gross Domestic Product (GDP).

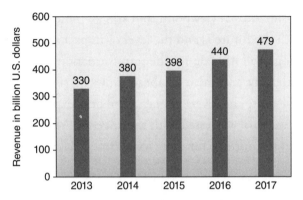

Note: Global revenue from smartphone sales from 2013–2017 (in billion U.S. dollars). Redrawn from Statista.[7]

- **Apple** is the inventor of the smartphone among many other things. Its revenues totaled $215 billion in 2017 and the company is worth around a trillion dollars. It has 123 000 employees.

- **Alphabet** (Google's parent company) had revenues totaling $110 billion in 2017 with net profits of $12 billion. The company is worth around $800 billion. It has 80 000 employees.

- **Facebook** had revenues of around $40 billion in 2017 with net profits of 15 billion dollars. It is worth around $525 billion. The company has 2.2 billion users and 25 000 employees.

Obviously, we could keep hurtling statistics at you, but you probably already get the point: the new information economy is VERY BIG BUSINESS. Companies like Apple and Amazon are worth about as much as the Italian gross domestic product—and the size of the entire global information economy in terms of annual revenues is now estimated to be $2–$3 trillion. What we are talking about here is an industry that connect literally billions of people to a wide range of web-based services. In doing so, they have built business empires that rival the economic output of the UK or Germany. And when it comes to competing for your digital dollars, these business people are not playing cricket. Not with each other, and certainly not with the rest of us!

Social Media: The Global Village

Social media, anyone? No, make that social media, *everyone*—according to Statista there are around 3 billion users of social media globally. Facebook is, of course the largest, with around 2 billion users a month.[8] According to Statista, the average global social media user spends more than two hours a day connected to their social media platforms, and Google now processes more than 40 000 searches a second—that's 3.5 billion searches a day or 1.2 trillion searches annually. What is unprecedented is that more people than ever existed cumulatively before the year 1800 now use the most advanced technology ever created *without paying a penny for it!* How does that work? The equation is actually very simple if you look at it as a reversal of the traditional vendor–consumer relationship. Your attention is the commodity that Google, Facebook, Instagram, Snapchat, Tinder and their peers buy and sell, and user interfaces (social medial and other apps) "bottle" your attention and resell it to advertisers.

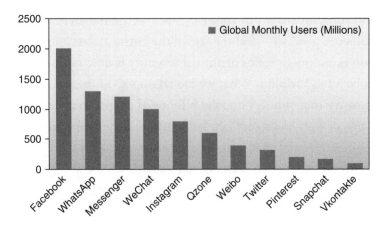

The fact of the matter is that we all *do* pay for using these platforms—with our attention! Sadly, many if not most of us are completely unaware of how valuable the power of attention and the ability to concentrate and focus is to our quality of life. Of course, attention in this respect has always been a commodity on some level; it precedes everything else your employer pays you for. Unfortunately, never in history have there been so many demands for attention made on the human brain, nor has brain and behavioral science ever been so powerful in the hands of MBAs (Master of Business Administration). All of which have huge ramifications for human society.

And now we're at the crux of our first chapter: The global market for buying and selling human attention online is worth nearly a *trillion* dollars a year—obviously every player in the market will go a very long way to ensure that you remain interested in their offerings—and, just as obviously, your choice of smartphone or tablet is worth a lot of money to tech manufacturers.

Netflix CEO Reed Hastings has claimed that the streaming giant's biggest rivals aren't Amazon, YouTube or even traditional broadcasters. According to Hastings, our need for sleep is actually its main barrier. "You know, think about it, when you watch a show from Netflix and you get addicted to it, you stay up late at night," he has said. "We're competing with sleep, on the margin. And so, it's a very large pool of time."[9]

Meanwhile Google aims to make its services increasingly ubiquitous and to remove the barriers caused by the use of a device. "Looking to the future, the next big step will be for the very concept of the 'device' to fade away," Google CEO Sundar Pichai says. "Over time, the computer itself—whatever its form factor—will be an intelligent assistant helping you through your day. We will move from mobile first to an AI first world."[10]

The inherent danger, obviously, is that when technology becomes too much of a crutch, it makes you "lazy." Before the advent of smartphones, most of us could hold 20 or even 50 phone numbers in our head. The same goes for how GPS kills your ability to find your way using a regular map. In other words, relying on technology to do sorting and reasoning tasks that you can do on your own will eventually decrease your own ability to do them. This digital outsourcing of our cognitive skills is actually described in the "extended mind theory," which is an idea in the field of philosophy of mind often called "extended cognition." The theory holds that the reach of the mind need not end at the boundaries of skin and skull. Tools, instruments and other environmental props such as our beloved smartphones can under certain conditions also count as proper parts of our minds.[11]

But unfortunately, the old bodybuilder adage goes for your brain as well: "use it or lose it." Daniel Wegner, a Harvard professor and senior author of a recent study on how being online affects human memory, believes that the Internet has become "part of a transactive memory source, a method by which our brains compartmentalize information." According to Wegner, transactive memory exists in many forms, as when a husband relies on his wife to remember a relative's birthday. "[It is] this whole network of memory where you don't have to remember everything in the world yourself," he says. "You just have to remember who knows it." Now computers and technology as well are becoming virtual extensions of our memory.[12,13]

It is important to remember that one main distinction from former "mind extension tools" like phone books, maps or text books from the past is that they were simple tools for set purposes, requiring a specific amount of mental resources. You didn't get distracted by your phone book or led astray on purpose by your map.

Tackling the Onslaught of Information

Most people have heard of Moore's Law—the idea that the speed and capacity of computers doubles roughly every 18 months. But what about Amdahl's Law, a formula used to calculate the theoretical speedup of a computing system when using multiple processors to do calculations? As it happens, Amdahl's law can also be applied to interactions between humans and computers. According to researchers Randolph Bias, Douglas Gillan and Clayton Lewis,

> Amdahl's Law demonstrates, algebraically, that increasingly the (non-parallelizable) human performance becomes the determining factor of speed and success in most any

human-computer system. Whereas engineered products improve daily, and the amount of information for us to potentially process is growing at an ever quickening pace, the fundamental building blocks of human information processing (e.g., reaction time, short-term memory capacity) have the same speed and capacity as they did for our grandparents. Or, likely, for the ancient Greeks.[14]

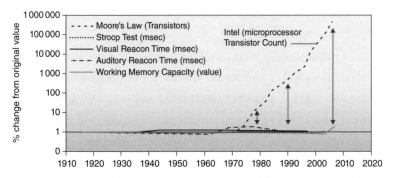

Note: Human-information processing variables compared with Moore's law data. Reproduced with permission. Redrawn from Bias et al. (2014)[15]

The graph shows Moore's law (the dash line) versus the overall human ability to process information (the other lines). As should be readily apparent, computers may help provide access to more information, but they do not make us better at processing information and we can't seem to keep up the pace.[16]

This poses a challenge: If you can only absorb and respond to a certain amount of information every day and you're constantly confronted with a much larger amount of information than you can digest, how do you decide where best to invest your capacity to absorb information?

Obviously, the providers of social media and smartphones want you to spend as much time as possible online because that's how they make their money. But just because social media providers want it doesn't mean you have to give it to them. The choice is yours and maybe there are better things you could be investing your time in. On top of that you might be surprised to learn that time spent online may also diminish your power to concentrate and reason— even when you're *not* online.

In other words, even though we now get more information thrown at us faster and faster, we do not automatically get better or faster at absorbing or interacting with this information. To make things worse, when people's jobs and careers increasingly depend on using this fairly limited information processing ability to process ever increasing amounts of information, it may explain why mental health problems are on the rise in most of the Western world.

Notes

1. https://www.mediapost.com/publications/article/291358/90-of-todays-data-created-in-two-years.html

2. https://techcrunch.com/2010/08/04/schmidt-data/

3. https://www.gartner.com/newsroom/id/2636073

4. *Ericsson Mobility Report June 2018*. Retrieved from https://www.ericsson.com/assets/local/mobility-report/documents/2018/ericsson-mobility-report-june-2018.pdf.

5. https://www.technologyreview.com/s/609232/the-surgeon-who-wants-to-connect-you-to-the-internet-with-a-brain-implant/

6. https://www.theguardian.com/technology/2017/feb/15/elon-musk-cyborgs-robots-artificial-intelligence-is-he-right

7. Statista. *Smartphone sales revenue worldwide 2013-2017.* https://
www.statista.com/statistics/237505/global-revenue-from-
smartphones-since-2008/

8. https://infographic.statista.com/normal/chartoftheday_5194_
active_users_of_social_networks_and_messaging_services_n.jpg

9. https://www.independent.co.uk/life-style/gadgets-and-tech/news/
netflix-downloads-sleep-biggest-competition-video-streaming-ceo-
reed-hastings-amazon-prime-sky-go-a7690561.html

10. http://time.com/4311233/google-ceo-sundar-pichai-letter/

11. https://en.wikipedia.org/wiki/The_Extended_Mind

12. https://harvardmagazine.com/2011/11/how-the-web-affects-
memory

13. https://www.scientificamerican.com/article/internet-transactive-
memory/

14. https://www.researchgate.net/publication/265413054_The_Tortoise
_and_the_Software_Moore%27s_Law_Amdahl%27s_Law_and_
Performance_Trends_for_Human-_Machine_Systems?_sg=_
eG79o9bIGPvz063pPl5rE004IUEKQGFc2C3Gvpl1N76bId2
UwGe1_F_aNUUggukOJFClk5CWw

15. Bias, R.G., Lewis, C. Gillan, D. The Tortoise and the (Soft)ware:
Moore's Law, Amdahl's Law, and Performance Trends for
Human-Machine Systems. *The Journal of Usability Studies, Vol 9*(4),
129-151. http://uxpajournal.org/the-tortoise-and-the-software-
moores-law-amdahls-law-and-performance-trends-for-human-
machine-systems/

16. https://www.researchgate.net/publication/265413054_
The_Tortoise_and_the_Software_Moore%27s_Law_Amdahl%27s_
Law_and_Performance_Trends_for_Human-_Machine_Systems?_sg
=_eG79o9bIGPvz063pPl5rE004IUEKQGFc2C3Gvpl1N76bId2U
wGe1_F_aNUUggukOJFClk5CWw

Chapter Two

A Fire Upon the Deep[1]

In his much acclaimed book, *Sapiens*,[2] Yuval Harari points
out that humans are a social species by design as much as by
choice; in other words, social behavior is actually written
into our biology. Harari suggests that the taming of fire was
the trigger that would eventually lead to the development
of language, cognition and social skills. Fire allowed early
humans to survive in unfriendly environments. Being able
to cook food instead of eating it raw meant fewer infections
and less time spent eating and digesting. Fire gave us control
over our surroundings. Armed with fire, even the most
fragile members of the tribe could burn down a whole forest
in no time and, once the fire had died down, could harvest
large amounts of everything from torched animals to nuts
and kernels.

Being able to eat more in less time and gaining access
to more opportunity is believed to have slowly changed our
biology over a period of about one hundred thousand years.
We no longer needed a Herculean muscle mass and sharp teeth
just to get through an ordinary day in the jungle or forest.
This freed up nutritional resources that were better invested

in the power of cognition. Gradually, we became more agile and flexible creatures with bigger brains.

Michael Tomasello, Esther Hermann et al. proposed the cultural intelligence hypothesis in 2005,[3] a theory that elaborates on how the human brain developed intelligence a lot faster and more effectively than any other primate on the planet through a couple of mediating processes that was partially based on culture and the social nature of mankind.

Whereas primates in general have evolved sophisticated social-cognitive skills for better competition and cooperation purposes, humans—being ultra-social—evolved additional skills, which enabled us to create specific cultural groups, each operating with a distinctive set of artifacts, symbols, social practices and institutions. To function effectively within the cultural context, human children must learn to use these artifacts and tools through more or less formalized learning processes.

This requires special social-cognitive skills of learning, communication and bonding and this especially powerful and early use of social-cultural cognition is proposed to serve as a kind of "bootstrap" or mediating process for the distinctively complex development of human cognition in general. Again, yet another ramification of why the human brain is highly susceptible to anything that triggers our socially wired brain patterns.

Developing Bigger Brains Was an Evolutionary Gamble

There was a trade-off to getting a bigger brain. On one hand, it made us better at hunting, gathering, figuring things out, planning ahead, communicating and organizing ourselves into groups, clans, tribes and eventually societies. But it also meant danger and added risk. Bigger brains meant bigger heads and thus an increased risk of mother and/or child dying during birth. Furthermore, getting that big brain to work properly meant that children needed many years of nurturing before reaching self-sufficiency. In turn, arose the need to organize ways in which children and parents could remain together and could remain safe over long periods of time. Quite a few anthropologists (in particular in the field of biological anthropology) believe that this dependency created "social brains."[4]

Our understanding of human evolution is to a large extent based on looking at what our ancestors left behind (including their skulls!). Mapping the modern, conscious human brain is a puzzle game for anthropologists, archaeologists and sociologists trying to understand the thought processes behind the artifacts left behind.[5] One thing that most researchers agree on, however, is that symbolic thinking—the ability to imagine things—is crucial to the development of conscious thought and the development of modern humanity. What we do know is that Homo sapiens apparently first appeared in East Africa around 150 000 years ago. Back then, we were a fairly inconsequential species, but around 70 000 years ago an extraordinary cognitive revolution erupted.

It's hard to pinpoint exactly when the modern human brain actually evolved. Is our ability to think and reason a function of possessing language or are there other factors involved? After all, many species of animals have some sort of language. Current anthropological and paleoanthropological[6] thinking has identified different factors that when brought together may have been the basis for the emergence of human consciousness and cognition:

- The need to warn or orient other members of your group. For example, green monkeys can warn each other of an approaching lion.[7]

- The need for sharing information about the internal workings of groups (hierarchies, ranking of groups, social strata) as a means of giving birth to more complex language.

- The ability to imagine things that do not exist. The truly unique feature of human language is not its ability to transmit information about men and lions but to imagine things that do not exist at all; in other words, symbolic thinking.[8]

In a relatively brief span of time—by most estimates as little as 30 000 to 40 000 years—we Homo sapiens became cognizant, developed language and social skills, increased our life span, started travelling, and made a myriad of inventions (clothing, tools, weapons). We even developed a range of new intellectual concepts such as art, religion and trading. All of this took place because something just as stupendous was going on inside our skulls—the human brain was growing and adapting, getting larger, smarter and much more capable of solving problems, laying plans and using tools.

The Three Layers of Your Brain[9]

To fully appreciate the invasiveness of current brain-hacking techniques, it's helpful to learn a few brain basics. A good place to start is the triune brain model, formulated in the 1960s by neuroscientist Paul D. MacLean.[10] Although the model is highly simplified and in some details inaccurate and therefore a bit outdated, it still provides an easy-to-understand approximation of the hierarchy of brain functions. The triune model describes the brain as an inverted pyramid with three tiers, each of which formed as a response to a major evolutionary challenge requiring the brain to cope with increasingly complex demands.

The brain's three main components—the triune—developed independently of each other, starting with the most primitive layer that controls basic, involuntary functions and progressing to the most evolved layer, the one containing most of the functions that distinguishes humans from other animals. Although in terms of practical function the relationships among the three tiers of the brain are more complex and nuanced with areas of overlap, the model gives the essence of brain mechanics.

The nervous system, the brain stem, the deep nuclei and cerebellum came first. These parts of your brain run basic functions such as breathing and heart rate. They also manage features such as balance, motor skills and coordination.

Next came your limbic brain, also known as the mammal brain, which manages emotions and feelings (including anxiety and the fight–flight–freeze response).

While all of this came early, your neocortical brain with its frontal lobes (sometimes also known as your cerebrum) probably came somewhat later in the history of human evolution. This is the part of your brain that enables you to speak, think, solve problems, remember phone numbers and so forth.

In essence, as you move through life, making decisions and checking your mail, driving your car or walking down steps, different neural operating systems are functioning simultaneously. Because these systems are mostly running on autopilot, you normally don't need to worry about them. Beneath the level of consciousness, your lower brain keeps you breathing while your higher brain keeps you in your lane.

The brain is brilliant in spontaneously rearranging its division of labor between layers. Learning is handled by the "newest" part of your brain, the neocortical brain and frontal lobes. But once the task is routine, its required actions are passed on to the cerebellum and deep nuclei where they can run on "autopilot."

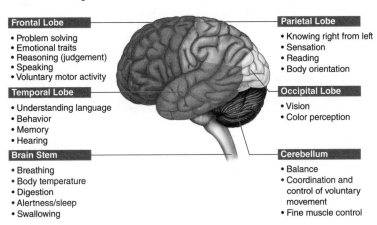

Frontal Lobe
- Problem solving
- Emotional traits
- Reasoning (judgement)
- Speaking
- Voluntary motor activity

Temporal Lobe
- Understanding language
- Behavior
- Memory
- Hearing

Brain Stem
- Breathing
- Body temperature
- Digestion
- Alertness/sleep
- Swallowing

Parietal Lobe
- Knowing right from left
- Sensation
- Reading
- Body orientation

Occipital Lobe
- Vision
- Color perception

Cerebellum
- Balance
- Coordination and control of voluntary movement
- Fine muscle control

This is why you can have a conversation while driving or practice the guitar while watching a movie. This is obviously a very practical feature of your brain. However, it is also a feature that can be "hacked" by the addictive design techniques

embedded in your smartphone or the notification stream
of your social media. More about that later in this book.[11]

So, it's clear that the mammalian brain evolved to such
an extent that it (happened to) meet an ever-shifting array
of mammalian needs. But what are these needs? Although
not without its critics, Maslow's hierarchy of needs is widely
accepted as a useful baseline for most discussions about
fundamental human necessities.[12]

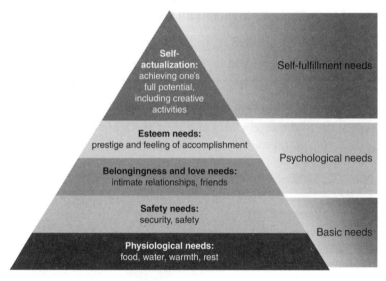

Recent research supports Maslow's core premise that we
experience a fulfilling and satisfying life when certain needs
are met. In 2011, for example, researchers from the University
of Illinois led a study[13] that put the hierarchy of needs to the
test worldwide. The researchers found that humans have
specific universal needs and that we feel we have achieved
fulfillment when these needs are met. Lead investigator Ed
Diener concluded:

> Our findings suggest that Maslow's theory is largely correct.
> In cultures all over the world the fulfilment of his proposed

needs correlates with happiness. However, an important departure from Maslow's theory is that we found that a person can report having good social relationships and self-actualization even if their basic needs and safety needs are not completely fulfilled.

In other words, close social ties and intimacy are needs, not accessories.

Interestingly, when the triune brain model and Maslow's hierarchy of needs are put side by side as shown on the opposite page, there seems to be a near-perfect match between the brain's three-tiered functionality and our three categories of needs. The brain's three tiers—the primal brain stem, the psycho-emotional limbic system and the super-egoic neocortex—neatly reflect Maslow's three categories of need.

Your experience of basic needs being met is felt through impulses, reflexes and hormones and regulated mostly below conscious control. The emotional needs, met by the "emotional brain" experiencing a rise in certain hormonal levels, make us feel that we are loved or cared about. Finally, the need for self-fulfillment is in many ways the product of thought processes coming from the high-level functions that allow us to plan ahead and undertake complex analytical thought processes.

One reason that social media has the power to absorb and engage us is that it mimics the fulfillment of many social needs. However, mimicking fulfillment of social needs is not the same as actually fulfilling those needs: digital "fake socialization" fails to deliver a sufficient rise in the brain's level of hormones, needed to create the actual feeling of belonging or being loved. Especially in younger people whose social skills are still being formed, social media mimicking can supplant the necessity of taking the real-life emotional risks necessary to reach intimacy

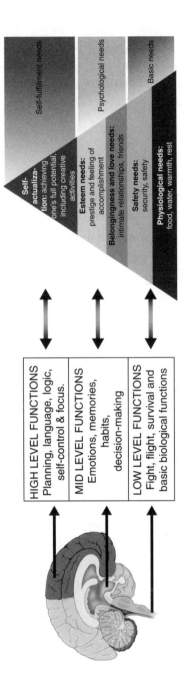

with others, making it even harder to develop the necessary social skills to be used in the physical world.

Moreover, as anyone with about five minutes' experience with digital communications knows, heavy use of texting to communicate feelings in a relationship can go off track quickly and badly. In fact, researchers have found that if you text too much with your partner, there might be less satisfaction in the relationship, especially if you are male. This texting study also concluded that:

> There is a large body of research indicating that negative communication can have an absorbing effect in a relationship and ultimately lead to destabilization and eventual dissolution, so setting up a ratio of positives to negatives is a way to counteract those effects. And since verbal and facial cues are an incremental part of communication, and these cues are missing in non-vocal types of communication, such as texting and emailing, partners may misconstrue messages and attribute emotional meaning that is absent, because emotional cues are often intuited from vocal inflection. Clinicians can use this information to encourage clients to be mindful and purposeful about the content of messages sent in romantic relationships, and to be slow to interpret meaning in technology communications.[14]

In other words: make sure that you don't let heart emojis get in the way of showing real human affection because it simply doesn't fill that need.

As with other potentially addictive or compulsive activities, the context in which you engage in it can make all the difference. To wit, a 2017 Duke University study published in the journal *Current Directions in Psychological Science*[15] found that college students' experience of technology, be it positive or negative, had less to do with *how much* they used it than it did with *how* they used it.

The researchers found that college freshmen were mainly using Facebook to keep in touch with their friends from high school, and the more time they spent online, the less time they had for building new friendships on campus. This inevitably led to increased feelings of loneliness. In contrast, college seniors were using Facebook mainly to communicate with friends *on* campus. So, the more time they spent online, the more connected they felt. And while there are clear drawbacks to allowing the digital world to become one's primary point of contact with humanity, we are not completely defenseless. One of our best weapons against this mental army of occupation is awareness of our intention.

The fact is, our analog brain isn't wired for the concept of "digital friendships." Being online does not allow us to read social cues and bond the way we evolved to do in the physical presence of others. It is true that when you engage in social media, the brain ticks off a box in the social relations category. But it's a little like someone whose health relies on a certain medication, but the person is given sugar pills by mistake. The placebo effect may carry them along for a while, but if the medication is essential, the body will eventually start to break down. Just as is the case with what you actually get out of social media interactions.

In essence you are being tricked into thinking you've gotten something you urgently need—but without having actually obtained it. The "it" in this case being nothing less than human connection. It's like trying to water a plant with a picture of water or paying a bill by jangling change.

Digital communication typically doesn't allow you to see, feel or even sense the other person you just interacted with, yet your brain has marked the need to do this down as "accomplished."

Obviously if you have few or no friends at all, then surely having friends online is better than no friends at all. And of course, it's also true that the kind of social relations that people form online surely can fill some of the need for contact with other humans—however, it's important that we don't forget the obvious: humans need humans. Not by choice, but by evolutionary design. Our powerful psychological and emotional needs are an inherent part of our humanity.

Our hierarchy of needs starts with the elemental substances like water and food. Moving up the pyramid we ascend to the psycho-emotional realm with our need for love and affection. And finally, we wind up with the more sublime concept of "self-actualization," meaning that we can now set our sights beyond our own immediate need for survival and project our energies into creative, altruistic or more universal considerations.

We can agree on a certain baseline of needs merely to sustain a beating heart: water, a certain number of calories, protection from food and cold. But step one yard outside the iron circle of strict biological sustenance, and the word "need" becomes very subjective. Whether or not one's needs are being met can be a matter of perception: does one "need" a certain kind of car, a certain amount of space to live in, a gym membership, or for that matter a better smartphone?

Because our sense of "need" is largely conditioned, it can be reconditioned. On the Internet, we will always be convinced of needs we didn't know we had. Et voila! A new item—on sale!—will suddenly appear to match this need. There is also the encouragement to "share" your purchase online, which means that if your peer group engages in such exhibitionism, you may be persuaded that your lack of the Bird Man Hybrid Jetpack recently acquired by three of your friends (that you've never met personally) is a tragic injustice.

Facebook has been shown strongly to trigger and reinforce social comparison, a psychological trait that biases you toward perceiving superior traits in others. This naturally evokes negative feelings of inferiority, envy and depression, according to a 2017 review of research on social media usage quoted by the *Harvard Business Review*.[16] Of course, media in general and social media in particular are powerful reinforcers of popular notions about attractiveness and other aspects of the desire realm.

But today's digital user gets it from all sides: glimpses into the "lives" of others that may look more attractive than one's own, followed by a left hook in the form of banner ads and biased search returns that continually shrink our horizons by anticipating and reinforcing our desires.

Other research cited by the Association for Psychological Science has found:

- The more time you spend on Facebook and the more actual strangers you have as Facebook friends, the more likely you are to feel that others have got better lives than you do.[17]

- In daily diary research, more time spent on Facebook was associated with more social comparison, which was in turn associated with higher levels of depression; reversed models that attempted to treat depression as the mediator between Facebook use and social comparison did not fit the data.[18]

- People who are more likely overall to compare themselves with others are both more likely to use Facebook and more likely to suffer from lower self-esteem after Facebook use.[19]

- Experimental work also confirms that comparing oneself with superior others' profiles on social network sites can result in greater dissatisfaction with one's achievements.[20]

While it is true that "self-esteem" is an intangible and that any measurement of it is based on subjective reporting, low self-esteem as well as real or perceived threats to one's self-image is correlated to the amount of cortisol—the stress hormone—present in your body. This brings us to a little talked about part of the brain known as the hypothalamic pituitary adrenal, or HPA, axis, which regulates the body's stress response and release of cortisol and other stress hormones.

Researchers have only recently begun to look into the interplay between digital behavior and the HPA axis, but in one study they were able to show that "body shaming" and negative physical social comparisons measurably triggered cortisol response and HPA axis activity in 44 healthy students.[21]

What's more, it seems likely to emerge that giving young children a free hand with smartphones and tablets could set them up for stress problems later in life. A 2014 study in the journal *Psychoneuroendocrinology* found that young children who suffer social isolation—which overuse of digital devices can certainly engender—may sustain permanent damage to their HPA axis and experience difficulties coping with stress later in life.[22]

As noted, research into social media and stress reveals some opposing and sometimes contradictory threads. It's hard to know in what proportions one's relationship to digitalia is a projection of the user or a function of the medium manipulating the user. But it's easy to see how constant engagement, especially for younger people, could reinforce isolation in those who already have a tendency toward it.

Children whose self-image is still being formed and who may suffer from normal transitional insecurities are vulnerable for obvious reasons; Facebook use has indeed been shown both to enhance healthy social habits as well as exaggerate bad ones. But it's one thing to solidify one's sense of self on a school playground and quite another to do it amidst an onslaught of wishfully constructed personality profiles in a never-ending pageant of faux self-satisfaction.

According to social self-preservation theory, the HPA axis is a key part of the individual's social self-preservation system, the job of which is to scan the environment for threats to social status or social esteem. Threats trigger both cortisol production and negative thought-streams and emotions.

"Given that Facebook use has been associated with social status and social esteem," speculates the journal *Frontiers in Psychology*, "it is possible that Facebook use could be viewed as a threat to self-preservation and may induce similar physiological effects."[23]

This comment was in relation to a study in which participants were asked to engage with their own Facebook profile immediately after being dealt an acute social stressor.

These people experienced "significantly higher levels of objective stress compared to control participants (i.e. their recovery from stress was delayed)." The study surmised that the stress was in response to the perception that one's self-preservation was under attack.

It is clear that living with a smartphone as a quasi-extension of self is like having a huge bundle of exposed nerves growing out of your palm; the additional stimuli that you absorb are going to keep your fight or flight response perpetually triggered. The constant self-generated pressure to check calls, notifications and alerts, texts, social media tags and email keeps the adrenal glands in a constant state of agitation. This, along with spikes in cortisol, is a recipe for heart disease and numerous other mortal pathologies. And we're only beginning to contemplate the long-term implications. It is quite possible that we'll see a continuing rise in heart-related problems as these cortisol spikes lead to an avalanche of issues including high blood pressure, increased heart rate and anxiety.

None of this, of course, is going to improve anyone's overall mental performance or sense of well-being.

Prefiltering and Neuroplasticity: Your Adaptable Brain

Every second of the day, your brain is bombarded by a staggering amount of information, a process also known as sensory input. This information stream is so massive that your brain's processing power cannot cope with all of it. To deal with this overflow, the brain has developed two different coping mechanisms: prefiltering and neuroplasticity.

The first term, prefiltering, is an autonomous process that has a couple of important functions. Not only is most of your sensory input filtered without any conscious interaction, it also allows you to categorize your sensory inputs in larger and meaningful parts to make it easier to process information about the world around you. It's a bit like your own mental overload protection. But it was not designed to protect you against the kind of mind hacking that we'll be discussing later.

The second term, neuroplasticity,[24] covers the biological processes that keep your brain centers renewed, allowing some new nerve cells to be created but mostly keeping existing nerve cells active and fully functional[25] by continuously revising the connections between nerve cells. Neuroplasticity also enables your brain to create new connections and networks—in essence to rewire itself to an almost unbelievable degree. And as we'll see in later chapters of this book, the businesses that target and resell your attention have a vested interest in exploiting this rewiring capability to get you hooked on their products.

Your brain contains about 86 billion nerve cells, of which 16–19 billion are in the cerebral cortex. Each nerve cell sprouts as many as 10 000 connections to other nerve cells, the so-called synapses. Researchers believe that information is encoded in your brain via the connection patterns within the individual networks of nerve cells in the brain. Theoretically, it means that each brain cell can connect in an inconceivably enormous number of different ways. If you multiply 20 billion cells with the ability to connect in more than 10 000 ways, the result is a level of complexity that is almost unfathomable. Yet, as cognizant humans we take all this for granted and spend little time thinking about it.[26]

Is Your Consciousness Time-Shifted?

In his book, *The User Illusion—Cutting Consciousness Down to Size*,[27] Tor Nørretranders explains just how little of our own supposed "consciousness" we actually control.[28] Our sensory devices (eyes, ears, smell, taste, tactility) generate huge amounts of data. This data first gains entry through the subconscious parts of the brain where the already-mentioned prefiltering takes place and data is processed and sorted, after which only one part in a million is forwarded to your "consciousness." This separating of the relevant from the irrelevant takes place entirely without any conscious interaction.[29]

Subconscious processes also play a dominant role in what you would normally consider conscious physical actions. In one famous study by Benjamin Libet,[30] subjects were wired with electrodes recording the electrical activity in their brain and then asked to look at a light moving up and down a pole with markers. They were told to bend their finger whenever they wished but to remember where on the pole the light was when they made the decision to bend their finger. Surprisingly, the experiment showed that electrical activity in the cortical areas of the brain began approximately half a second before the subjects watching the timer believed they had decided to trigger the movement.

This half-second delay—the "hesitation of consciousness"—gave rise to fierce discussion between researchers focusing on consciousness and neuroscience. Because when a touch on the skin is felt with virtually no delay, to claim that a time lapse occurs when you bend your finger didn't seem logical. However, this delay has since been further proven in electrical brain stimulation experiments during open skull operations and it is now clear that something is going on "under the hood," before we realize it "ourselves." Subconscious parts of your brain may already be in the process of acting before "you" become aware of it consciously.

According to Nørretranders, the explanation for this strange discrepancy is as spectacular as it is counter-intuitive: he—together with other researchers such as Libet—claims that everything we experience with our consciousness is an illusion. It's an illusion that has arisen because our subconscious brain doesn't just summarize our sensory input but also time-shifts it to make experienced sensation fit our conscious experience. The subconscious part of the brain censors and sequences reality for us and what seems to our consciousness to be going on in "real time" is in reality time-shifted by about half a second by subconscious processes in order to keep your consciousness running in sync with your sensory input. Another, less deterministic way to view our consciousness, would be to claim that every conscious thought starts as a subconscious signal, and that the generation of consciousness is the endpoint of cogitation that enables us to communicate our experiences to others and to learn from them ourselves.

Not everyone agrees with the idea of the "hesitation of consciousness" and the claim has been made that the subjects in the Libet study were not unaware of the task, even though they were free to choose a time to move. The task is foremost in their consciousness and constantly activates a series of possible neuronal actions, only one of which is recorded when they finally choose to act.

However, regardless of whether the "hesitation of consciousness" theory is right or not, there is little doubt that the subconscious processing and filtering function of our brains provides an explanation as to why our consciousness is so relatively easily won over by technologies that constantly seek our attention.[31]

To Be or Not to Be Conscious

The American philosopher and psychologist William James suggested[32] that people generally possess two types of "thinking": associative and reason-based. Associative thinking is reactive and based on past experiences while reason-based thinking is suited to situations where you lack experience and must reason your way to a decision. In his book *Thinking, Fast and Slow*, Nobel Memorial Prize-winning psychologist and economist Daniel Kahneman[33] and his associate Amos Tversky describe how we use these two different types of thought processes or systems when making decisions.[34] Kahneman researched these two systems extensively and has been able to show that your autopilot (what William James called "reactive thinking") makes "shortcuts" into areas where consciousness does not follow.[35] Your autopilot is constantly active. It sorts impressions and renders verdicts, but its judgments are based not on reason and analysis but on instincts and associations, and it often "shoots from the hip."[36]

For example, imagine that you are given a description of Simone and Bob. Simone is intelligent, diligent, impulsive, critical, stubborn and envious. Bob is envious, stubborn, critical, impulsive, diligent and intelligent. If you are like most people, you will immediately consider Simone more sympathetic than Bob. But the reality is that the two people were described in exactly the same words, just in a different order. This example demonstrates that the order of adjectives colors your overall experience because your fast-moving autopilot bases its judgments on associations and first-hand impressions. The first words are recorded as either positive or negative and then color the rest of the experience.[37]

According to Kahneman, in contrast to your "autopilot," the conscious part of your decision-making system is slow and lazy. It requires a lot of energy and discipline to operate. It keeps an eye on the autopilot and reflects on whether your automatic reactions or "gut feelings" are inappropriate or problematic. Its tasks are all characterized by the need for attention and resources, such as analyzing the data on an Excel sheet, making business decisions or value-based choices.

In modern cognition and consciousness research it is noteworthy that the two different thought processes for practical reasons are named the reflective and pre-reflective self-consciousness, indicating that you are always conscious to some extent, but the difference between the two states is whether or not you reflect on *what* you're conscious about.[38]

Out of Control

Recently the American professor of psychology Ezequiel Morsella proposed a theory of consciousness in line with Kahneman and Nørretranders but describing consciousness as being far more automated and far less purposeful than previously assumed. Morsella's passive frame theory, based on 10 years of research and testing, suggests that the conscious mind is like an interpreter helping speakers of different languages communicate. "The interpreter presents the information but is not the one making any arguments or acting upon the knowledge that is shared," Morsella said. "Similarly, the information we perceive in our consciousness is not created by conscious processes, nor is it reacted to by conscious processes. Consciousness is the middle-man, and it doesn't do as much work as you think."[39]

According to Morsella, the "free will" that people typically attribute to their conscious mind—the idea that our consciousness acts as "decider" and guides us to a course of action—does not exist. Instead, consciousness only relays information to control "voluntary" action or goal-oriented movement involving the skeletal muscle system.

Another way to understand Morsella's theory is to use the Internet as an analogy. Here you can buy books, book hotel rooms and do thousands of other things. But in reality, the Internet does not do anything on its own. It is the user behind the screen or smartphone who decides what to do. The Internet simply performs the actions it was originally designed and programmed to perform. The concept of "free

will" is based on the idea that your "consciousness" determines
what it wants to happen and then tries to make it happen.
But the truth is actually the reverse, according to Morsella. All
of the "planning" preceding a physical action is in fact taken
care of by parts of your brain that don't allow any conscious
control or input into this process! Because the human mind
experiences its own consciousness as a process of sifting
through urges, thoughts, feelings and physical actions, people
believe that their consciousness is in control of these myriad
impulses. But in reality, Morsella argues, consciousness does
the same simple task over and over, giving the impression that
it is doing more than it actually is. "We have long thought
consciousness solved problems and had many moving parts,
but it's much more basic and static," Morsella said. "This
theory is very counterintuitive. It goes against our everyday
way of thinking."[40]

According to Morsella, the reason for this is straightfor-
ward. As you know, the newest part of the human brain is just
a few hundred thousand years old. As with all other animals,
the more primitive part of the brain manages the reflexes and
instincts that keep us breathing, tell us to run when we're
threatened, tell us that we're hungry or thirsty, or that it's time
for a nap. These primal functions are constant and need not
burn energy by burdening the higher brain with analysis.

However, as humans became more complex and social
beings, as we began to speak, feel, use tools and, in general,
interact in a more reasoned way with our world, new brain
functions were required and these manifested as overlays on
top of existing brain parts, each improving the species' chances
for survival by making us more adaptable to our environments.

In other words, the development of these brain functions that we call "higher brain functions," is in reality just an adaptation function. They're simple extensions that the primitive brain has developed in order to carry out required thoughts or actions faster or more easily. However, the heaviest part of the work is done long before "consciousness" and the "higher brain functions" kick in. One of Morsella's explanations for our difficulty in understanding the function of consciousness is that we simply are not conscious enough to understand the explanation or its implications on our behavior.

Is Consciousness a Question of Being in the Spotlight?

Bernard J. Baars, a senior fellow at the Neurosciences Institute in La Jolla, California, offers a different model to help us understand how consciousness acts to match conscious and subconscious processes. His model, global workspace theory,[41] can be explained in terms of a "theater metaphor."

> In the "theater of consciousness" a "spotlight of selective attention" shines a bright spot on stage. The bright spot reveals the contents of consciousness, actors moving in and out, making speeches or interacting with each other. The audience is not lit up—it is in the dark (i.e. subconscious) watching the play. Behind the scenes and also in the dark, are the director (executive processes), stage hands, script writers, scene designers and the like. They shape the visible activities in the bright spot but are themselves invisible.[42]

In other words, consciousness is a constant flow of presence and information but is only available to us as self-understood consciousness when directed onto a particular

item or task. Interestingly, both the Morsella and the Baars
models are capable of accounting for how information flows
between consciousness and subconscious processes—between
our new neocortex and our older cerebellum and limbic
systems—between what Kahneman labels as respectively
"slow" and "fast" thinking.

Models Are Not Reality

The models presented by Nørretranders, Kahneman, Morsella
and Baars all deal with the issues of how consciousness man-
ifests and how cognitive processes rely on being able to shift
back and forth between different processing modes in the
brain. But these models do not represent "truth" as much as
they are models conceived by our own limited human brains,
and they are designed to explain phenomena we can observe
and measure. The best models are "good" because they deliver a
high degree of predictability and help explain our observations
in a way that supports further investigation.

It's easy to see that frames of reference and models are
extremely valuable tools. They help us understand the world
around us. Imagine sitting at a wooden table and letting
your hands glide over the surface, feeling the smoothness
of the grain. But what are you really "feeling" and how are
you "interpreting" what you feel or sense? A physicist could
argue that the table is just a cloud of loosely connected atoms.
Or a quantum physicist could argue that the table you "see"
is just a stream of photons that might have resided on the
Moon a nanosecond earlier. The point is that the "models" are
simply tools for describing phenomena, but they are not the
phenomena themselves. The model can be scaled to match
a particular point of view. This also applies to the cognitive

models presented by Nørretranders, Kahneman, Morsella and Baars. They are merely explanatory models—they represent a way of describing reality, but they are not "reality" as such.

Still, we find them useful for shedding light on what researchers believe is going on inside our head. What these models show is that there is still much that we do not understand about how we think and what consciousness really is. This understanding should perhaps make us become just a little more careful about how we use technology and to what extent we allow it to engage cognitive processes that are beyond the reach of our consciousness.

Complicated? It's about to get even worse. The models on cognitive processes and consciousness that we have discussed in this chapter are complex but at least they deal with what we can observe and share and hence discuss and form opinions about. But we are about to dive even deeper into the rabbit hole—into that which we know exists but cannot prove …

The Hard Question of Consciousness

David Chalmers is a neuroscientist and a professor of philosophy at the Australian National University. Known for his definition of the "hard problem of consciousness," Chalmers claims that the various models of consciousness all deal with "easy questions" but fail to answer the equally crucial but much more difficult question of *why* and *how* "phenomenal experiences" are created by our awareness of sensory information. Or as Chalmers phrases it:

> Why is it that when our cognitive systems engage in visual and auditory information-processing, we have a visual or auditory experience: the quality of deep blue, the sensation

of middle C? How can we explain why there is something it
is like to entertain a mental image, or to experience an
emotion? It is widely agreed that experience arises from a
physical basis, but we have no good explanation of why and
how it so arises. Why should physical processing give rise to
a rich inner life at all? It seems objectively unreasonable that
it should, and yet it does.[43]

Chalmers claims that consciousness is something more
than the biological or sociological rails that provide it, and that
the nature of consciousness may not be open to inspection,
understanding or modeling. He has characterized his view
as "naturalistic dualism": naturalistic because he believes
mental states are *caused* by physical systems (such as brains);
dualist because he believes that the created mental state (e.g.
consciousness) is distinct from and not reducible to the
physical systems that create it.[44] For readers interested in
this distinction (and it is fascinating stuff) looking up the
term "qualia" is recommended. The *Stanford Encyclopedia of
Philosophy* has a good review of the concept.[45] ☺

The Social Brain

We humans are extremely social creatures who thrive when
surrounded by others. This desire for social inclusion and
interpersonal exchange is what made us adapt to social media
so avidly and rapidly. Now, barely into our second decade since
the advent of social media, evidence is emerging that makes
it clearer than ever that our inborn sociability is deeply wired
into our brains and this makes us vulnerable to certain appeals
based on our sociability. Traveling salesmen have known this
since long before the days of the Silk Road, but the man selling

vacuum cleaners had neither the science nor the technology to literally hack into your brain.

In the past several years, even more evidence has emerged to show how our brain's architecture supports human evolutionary development, particularly in the form of our complex social behaviors.

The human brain as a whole is much larger than in any other mammal or primate of equivalent size. The brain's outermost layer, the neocortex, is particularly outsized, and that's the dashboard for our sociability. That evolution has allowed us to become social animals tells us that it is a survival trait, as was the development of brains that could reason, solve problems, develop tools, learn math and eventually figure out how to build airplanes, submarines, smartphones, satellites, laptops and so on.[46]

Although we cannot know for sure, the most likely explanation for the development of the social brain is that it evolved into a bigger brain with more flexibility. Bigger brains mean giving birth to children who need many years of rearing before they are able to survive on their own. The development of socially monogamous pair bonds and the inclusion of paternal care (in opposition to many other species) provides the foundation for a society capable of rearing children over longer periods of times. Developing a "social brain" makes this easier and allows for society to become more complex, more multifaceted, more dynamic and flexible. When parents stay together to raise kids the risk of predation and infanticide drops, which in turn lifts the whole species' chance for survival. And when parents began long-term parenting, this required the development of new and more complex social skills than are needed by species that are not sociable.

It is almost certain that our collective capacity for social cohesion arose out of the social tools that evolved to support cooperative parenting. Being able to set up and live in complex social environments facilitated the development of larger social groups, extended families, clans and tribes, all of which promoted higher rates of survival and reproduction. And there is a feedback loop here: the more that heightened social interaction helps the species survive and prosper, the more our brains will develop along lines that deliver more and better social capabilities.

As Harari points out in his book *Sapiens,* our brain's ability to engage in complex social behaviors is the seed of our much larger group affiliations, from having a sense of neighborhood to being citizens of a nation. Our brains are wired to make us feel rewarded when we engage in social interaction and to feel sensations similar to physical pain when socially rejected. In a sense, evolution has provided us with the perfect brain that lets us live in an ever more crowded world—as well as the perfect brain for getting absorbed by smartphones and social media. Its obvious benefits aside, complex social cooperation comes at a price. First, there's the requirement of a long-term parental investment, which for humans continues far beyond childhood. Second, although many social skills can only be learned through peer activities during adolescence, parents still have crucial roles to play, protecting, sheltering and nurturing.

Or as Dr. Pascal Vrticka at the Max Planck Institute for Human Cognitive and Brain Sciences puts it:

> An individual's attachment style is a measure for the quality of his/her social bonds with others. It is crucially shaped through interactions with caregivers in early life, such as a child's parents. If others close to a child are responsive and caring, the child develops a secure attachment style. If they are unresponsive or inconsistent in their behaviour towards the child, however, the child develops an insecure, either avoidant or anxious attachment style. Once acquired, the attachment style of a person is believed to remain rather stable throughout the lifespan, and to even be transmitted from one generation to the next. It is therefore likely to circularly influence many of the steps involved in social brain development and skill acquisition during childhood, adolescence, and even adulthood.[47]

Notes

1. https://en.wikipedia.org/wiki/A_Fire_Upon_the_Deep—I couldn't help picking this subheading as a pointer to Vernor Vinge's marvelous 1993 Sci-Fi novel "A Fire Upon the Deep" which takes an almost semiotic approach to space opera.

2. http://www.ynharari.com/book/sapiens/

3. http://science.sciencemag.org/content/317/5843/1360

4. https://www.scientificamerican.com/article/social-network-size-linked-brain-size/

5. https://www.smithsonianmag.com/science-nature/the-earliest-known-artists-studio-111717198/

6. "**Paleoanthropology** or **paleo-anthropology** is a branch of archaeology with a human focus, which seeks to understand the early development of anatomically modern humans, a process known as hominization, through the reconstruction of evolutionary kinship lines within the family Hominidae, working from biological evidence (such as petrified skeletal remains, bone fragments, footprints) and cultural evidence (such as stone tools, artifacts, and settlement localities). The field draws from and combines paleontology, biological anthropology, and cultural anthropology." https://en.wikipedia.org/wiki/Paleoanthropology

7. http://geecologist.org/2017/06/sapiens/

8. http://geecologist.org/2017/06/sapiens/

9. https://en.wikipedia.org/wiki/Human_brain

10. https://en.wikipedia.org/wiki/Triune_brain

11. http://www.humanbrainfacts.org/human-brain-functions.php

12. http://www.academia.edu/4245484/Improving_Maslow_s_Hierarchy_of_Needs_New_Approach_to_needs_hierarchy

13. https://www.ncbi.nlm.nih.gov/pubmed/21688922

14. https://www.tandfonline.com/doi/full/10.1080/15332691.2013.836051?scroll=top&needAccess=true

15. http://journals.sagepub.com/doi/pdf/10.1177/0963721417730833

16. https://hbr.org/2017/04/a-new-more-rigorous-study-confirms-the-more-you-use-facebook-the-worse-you-feel

17. Chou, H.-T.G., & Edge, N. (2012). "They are happier and having better lives than I am": The impact of using Facebook on perceptions of others' lives. *Journal of Cyberpsychology, Behaviour, and Social Networking*, 15, 2.

18. Nguyen Steers, M.-L., Wickham, R.E., & Acitelli, L.K. (2014). Seeing everyone else's highlight reels: How Facebook usage Is linked to depressive symptoms. *Journal of Social and Clinical Psychology*, 33(8): 701–731.

19. Vogel, E.A., Rose, J.P., Okdie, B.M., Eckles, K., & Franz, B. (2015). Who compares and despairs? The effect of social comparison orientation on social media use and its outcomes. *Journal of Personality and Individual Differences*, 86: 249–256.

20. Haferkamp, N., & Krämer, N.C. (2011). Social comparison 2.0: examining the effects of online profiles on social-networking sites. *Cyberpsychol Behav Soc Netw.* 14(5): 309–314.

21. https://www.ncbi.nlm.nih.gov/pmc/articles/PMC5125296/—Role of shame and body esteem in cortisol stress responses

22. https://www.ncbi.nlm.nih.gov/pmc/articles/PMC4252479/—Social Deprivation and the HPA Axis in Early Development

23. Rus, H.M., & Tiemensma, J. (2017). Social media under the skin: Facebook use after acute stress impairs cortisol recovery. *Frontiers in Psychology* 19 September. https://doi.org/10.3389/fpsyg.2017.01609

24. https://en.wikipedia.org/wiki/Neuroplasticity

25. https://www.sciencenews.org/article/human-brains-make-new-nerve-cells-and-lots-them-well-old-age

26. https://en.wikipedia.org/wiki/Neuroplasticity

27. https://www.goodreads.com/book/show/106732.The_User_Illusion

28. https://en.wikipedia.org/wiki/Tor_N%C3%B8rretranders

29. http://www.kickerstudio.com/2009/02/review-the-user-illusion/

30. https://www.sciencedirect.com/science/article/pii/S1053810016302690

31. http://www.kickerstudio.com/2009/02/review-the-user-illusion/ https://archive.nytimes.com/www.nytimes.com/books/98/05/03/reviews/980503.03johnst.html?_r=2&oref=slogin&oref=slogin

32. https://en.wikipedia.org/wiki/Dual_process_theory

33. Kahneman won the Nobel Memorial Prize in economic sciences 2002 for his work related to rational choice models. https://www.nobelprize.org/mediaplayer/index.php?id=531

34. https://en.wikipedia.org/wiki/Dual_process_theory

35. https://www.information.dk/moti/anmeldelse/2013/04/se-dine-egne-illusioner

36. https://commons.wikimedia.org/wiki/File:Cognitive_Bias_ Codex_With_Definitions,_an_Extension_of_the_work_of_John_ Manoogian_by_Brian_Morrissette.jpg

37. http://mentalfloss.com/article/68705/20-cognitive-biases-affect-your-decisions

38. https://plato.stanford.edu/entries/self-consciousness-phenomenological/#PreRefSelCon

39. https://news.sfsu.edu/consciousness-has-less-control-believed-according-new-theory

40. https://news.sfsu.edu/consciousness-has-less-control-believed -according-new-theory

41. https://en.wikipedia.org/wiki/Global_workspace_theory

42. Blackmore, Susan (2002). "There Is No Stream of Consciousness". *Journal of Consciousness Studies.* **9** (5–6): 17–28.

43. http://consc.net/papers/facing.html

44. https://en.wikipedia.org/wiki/David_Chalmers

45. https://plato.stanford.edu/entries/qualia-knowledge/

46. https://www.huffingtonpost.com/pascal-vrticka/human-social-development_b_3921942.html

47. https://pvrticka.com/2018/03/15/evolution-of-the-social-brain-in-humans/

Chapter Three

The Billion Dollar Question

What motivates human beings? That's a question every marketeer and every company in the world would like the answer to. Understanding motivation is the key to shaping behavior, and once you can shape behavior, you are on the road to riches. As we saw in Chapter 2, the brain has two different modes of thinking—fast and slow (or the automated, impulsive and subconscious thinking and the conscious, reasoning, analytical thinking, if you will). A major difference between the two thinking modes is that the rational brain contains a crucial brain function called impulse control, which we will elaborate on later in this chapter.

Your two different modes of thinking can be triggered individually by external stimulation. What's more, the two modes of thinking do not respond to the same types of triggers. To jumpstart the slow part of your brain, try solving a puzzle, reading a book or listening to an interesting story. In other words, it takes effort and energy to trigger your analytical, rational, problem-solving thinking. By contrast, the fast-moving part of your brain is much easier to activate: all you have to do is "flash" something at it that triggers a response based on a prior experience. In some ways, your fast-thinking mode responds pretty much like someone with severe ADHD (Attention Deficit Hyperactivity Disorder): easily distracted by anything that looks good, sounds fun or creates associations with previous, pleasure-filled experiences.

If 100 different people were asked whether they liked or disliked a specific food, beer or band, it would be completely impossible to say why a person liked one thing or another. If you asked them, they probably couldn't tell you either. Most likely they would just say that what they like tastes good or feels good or sounds good. But what does that actually mean? Just like Pavlov's legendary dogs, who were trained to salivate at the sound of a bell once they'd learned to associate its ringing with food, certain parts of the human brain also tend to create preconfigured responses to triggers. Our propensity to do so is based on our sensory organs' ability to activate specific neurons that in turn trigger the release of specific chemicals into the brain.

This underlying mechanism—the one that can make your mouth water when you smell pizza or make your feet want to dance when you hear a song—is managed by your endocrine system, whose hormones make up a large part of your body's inner communication system.

While the nervous system uses neurotransmitters as chemical messengers, the endocrine system uses hormones. For our purposes, two particular substances are especially worth exploring: dopamine and oxytocin. One makes you pay attention to whatever you feel good about, while the other makes you feel good about social activities and about bonding with others.

Dopamine: Sex, Drugs, and Rock 'n' Roll?

You've probably heard of dopamine, known best as a "feel-good hormone[1]." In the past couple of decades, countless articles have focused on how to get a dopamine boost through food, sex, exercise, partying, drinking or even taking drugs. Dopamine has been widely portrayed as the fountain from which energy and happiness spring. However, evidence suggests that dopamine is actually more of an "expectation trigger" than a "reward trigger." In a Cambridge University study, neuroscientist Wolfram Schultz showed the result of repeatedly smacking up the brain with a trigger–reward combination: over time, the dopamine response diminishes, eventually wearing off.[2] Not just that, other studies show that while tasks you experience as rewarding initially lead to higher levels of dopamine and an increased focus on these tasks, after some time further increases in dopamine levels seem to have the opposite effect. Imagine eating chocolate. The first bite is wonderful, and you just MUST have the second, the third and probably even the fourth. But after that most people begin to find the idea of more chocolate less appealing. This is not because the chocolate has suddenly become less tasty but because at this point your increased levels of dopamine, derived from the reward-feeling elicited by eating chocolate, leads you to lose focus on eating chocolate and start looking for "something else." In other words, dopamine promotes initial reward experiences and reward expectations but does not keep your attention focused on the reward for very long.[3]

Gaming addiction is known to occur exactly because of this effect, hooking the player with an unpredictable pattern of rewards and fails that lead to significantly higher levels of dopamine than a consistently predictable pattern. That's why slot machines are so addictive—you anticipate winning, but you are not rewarded consistently, instead getting a number of "near-wins," such as three of the four bars that would have given you jackpot. This succession of near hits keeps the dopamine flowing, possibly leading to addiction. This effect is also why the never-ending scroll of social media newsfeeds can keep you riveted: you never know what's going to show up next in your feed and that uncertainty of outcome keeps the dopamine flowing.

When people use drugs such as amphetamine or cocaine, for a short period of time the brain's reward system will increase dopamine output by 10–20 times. However, as *Scientific American* journalist Ferris Jabr phrases it:

> Addictive substances keep the brain so awash in dopamine that it eventually adapts by producing less of the molecule and becoming less responsive to its effects. As a consequence, addicts build up a tolerance to a drug, needing larger and larger amounts to get high.

Those addicted to gambling seem to experience exactly the same:

> Just as substance addicts require increasingly strong hits to get high, compulsive gamblers pursue ever riskier ventures. Likewise, both drug addicts and problem gamblers endure symptoms of withdrawal when separated from the chemical or thrill they desire.[4]

Vaughan Bell, a neuroscientist at UCL (University College London) has also pointed out that the brain's use of dopamine is much more complex than just rewarding activities that are good for you.

Studies on roulette players[5] have recorded as much activity when punters lose money with a miserable near-miss as when they have an enjoyable win. In this case, dopamine seems not to be signaling pleasure but indicating how close you got to the reward and encouraging another attempt. This works well when success depends on skill but falsely compels us in games of chance.[6]

Oxytocin: Humans Need Humans

Given the importance of our sociability, it makes sense that connecting with others through nurturing and other supportive behaviors would have its own reward hormone. Say hello to oxytocin, often described as the "love hormone." Oxytocin is strongly involved in crucial biological processes such as childbirth, breastfeeding and sex and it also plays a significant role in social processes such as bonding, building trust, gaining empathy and nurturing relationships.

In 1977, the Bee Gees had a Number One hit with "How Deep Is Your Love?"[7] But the real question probably should have been "How High Is Your Oxytocin Level?" Plenty of studies have revealed that couples who fall in love and stay in love have higher oxytocin levels than couples who don't stay together for long. In other words a simple blood test may reveal a good deal about the chances for you staying together with your new boy- or girlfriend for more than six months! Researchers at the Gonda Brain Sciences Center in Israel[8] compared oxytocin levels between singles and newly formed couples. They found that new lovers had significantly higher oxytocin levels than singles, and that the couples who stayed together saw no decrease in their oxytocin levels when checked again six months later. Most significantly, the researchers showed that the oxytocin levels recorded at the first assessment of new couples were a pretty accurate predictor of who would split up and who would stay together!

Meanwhile at Harvard, researchers have been tracking[9] the physical and emotional well-being of about 800 people for more than 75 years. They conclude that "Good relationships keep us happier and healthier. It's not just the number of friends you have, and it's not whether or not you're in a committed relationship, it's the quality of your close relationships that matters." In other words, close relationships have a profound and positive effect on your health and well-being while the inability to maintain intimate bonds can cause physical and emotional distress.

So, building relationships is good for you and having high oxytocin levels helps you do so. But just how strong is this correlation? And what comes first: the high oxytocin level leading to stronger bonding—or the better bonding leading to higher oxytocin levels? Studies suggest that both things occur: higher oxytocin levels make bonding easier while a conscious effort to bond and build relationships also helps promote higher oxytocin levels. Researchers at Baylor College of Medicine found that a mother's oxytocin level is a strong predictor of how often she looks at her child—a factor that is known to be crucial for mother–child bonding. The researchers were also able to show that:

> Mothers who showed low/average oxytocin response demonstrated a significant decrease in their gaze toward their infants during periods of infant distress, while such change was not observed in mothers with high oxytocin

response. The findings underscore the involvement of oxytocin in regulating the mother's responsive engagement with her infant, particularly in times when the infant's need for access to the mother is greatest.[10]

Summing it all up, the neurotransmitter dopamine plays a powerful role in motivating the rewarding of individual behaviors, but it only works this way for a short span of time and it is *only* released if there is some sort of trigger that sets up an expectation of future reward. Drugs or activities that stimulate dopamine release are likely to be addictive.[11] And the hormone oxytocin promotes trust-building and social bonding and influences your long-term behavior in ways that help create couples and social groups.

Does Your Family Suffer from Technoference?

What does all this have to do with smartphones and social media usage? The answers (and there is more than one) are obvious. First, if you produce smartphones or build social networks, the better you can orchestrate dopamine and oxytocin release among your user base, the more of its attention you can grab. That's great for tech companies, but any number of people would object to having their brain chemistry tampered with, especially as a large body of evidence emerges that these interfaces may be deleterious to your health.

Second, there is the very real issue of what happens to children when they do not get enough attention. What any kid growing up both needs and wants is her or his parents' attention. If you are a parent, you know how just about every single action kids take is followed by "Look, Mom (or Dad)!"

But what happens in a world where the attention of kids and parents is constantly drifting away from each other and towards a screen? And yes, these are the screens where addictive digital design promotes a "stickiness" that keeps both you and your kids glued to the phone and constantly on the lookout for notifications and other reward triggers.

This issue of technology injecting itself into the bonding space of child–parent relations (or for that matter romantic or just friendly relationships) is known as "technoference" and it can have grave consequences, especially for children, who run a real risk of being socially under-stimulated. Numerous studies show that when kids are deprived of direct physical contact, attention and interaction, they have a high propensity for ending up with mental disorders involving a lack of empathy or difficulty connecting with others, in addition to many other very real impediments to social functioning.

Brandon McDaniel, who coined the term "technoference," is a parenting researcher who has spent years examining the impact of digital devices on family life.[12]

> Have you ever taken your child to the park and looked at the parents around you? What do you see? If you've managed to look up from your own device, you've probably seen a lot of parents looking down at their devices. Indeed, observational research has found that 35 percent of parents are on the phone for about 1 in every 5 minutes of playground time with their child.[13]

What McDaniel found was that technoference probably has profound impact on our family lives. Focusing on your device instead of on your kids makes it harder for you to read their cues correctly. It also often leads to responding inappropriately or more harshly than usual and to responding much too late to contact cues.

> In essence, letting devices create distractions between parents and kids can potentially negatively impact every aspect of parenting, leading you to be less in sync with your child's cues and to misinterpret your child's needs.[14]

Even worse, reducing kids' amount of close physical contact with parents can have serious future consequences. Children don't do what you tell them to, they do what they see you do. And if you show them that being in a relationship means being distant and constantly distracted by a tablet screen, that becomes their model for relationships. It's a model that they will adapt and eventually begin to use as their own. What's more, technoference may instill the notion that the screen is more real, or at least more urgent, than real-life interactions, or an instant escape hatch from reality. Or as McDaniel phrases it: "These distractions could have very real meaning for how the rising generation begins to see the world around them and what it means to love and be loved."[15]

The shifting balance of our hormonal drivers towards online activities combined with the resulting loss of attention to the "real" world and the lessening of physically present social bonding could have grave consequences. It's not hard to see how these trends could irreversibly damage future generations' ability to commit fully and deeply with others in the real world. By comparison, a smart phone's malleability to your own will makes reverting to it as a default mechanism all too easy.

Being Able to Defer Gratification Is Crucial

As we have seen, human behavior is determined by a number of different and often complex factors. The "old brain" is mostly controlled by subconscious impulses and is easily distracted by "short-term rewards" that are often selfish in nature. The "new brain" is better at learning new skills and forming enduring social relationships. Using the old brain is easier and requires less energy and effort than using the new brain,[16] but ultimately if you fail to develop the self-discipline needed to use the part of the brain that makes informed decisions, learns new skills and builds new relationships, you're going to run into a lot of trouble. And if we all decide to take refuge in the instant gratifications of the virtual world, it is doubtful how many more concert pianists, brain surgeons, mathematicians, physicists, Nobel Prize laureates or F1 drivers the world will produce.

The Stanford Marshmallow Experiment[17] of 1960 demonstrated how crucial it is for a child to develop self-control at an early age. In that experiment, 600 children were offered the choice between having a treat right now or waiting for 15 minutes in order to get two treats instead of one. While the vast majority tried to delay (only a small percentage had their single treat on the spot!), only a third of the kids succeeded in sweating it out long enough to get their bonus marshmallow. The importance of this behavior, however, would become increasingly evident over time as the researchers tracked their subjects well into adulthood. What they found was that the kids with enough impulse control to delay eating the marshmallow would over time end up with better exam scores and eventually better-paying jobs. Furthermore, a 2011 brain imaging study of a number of the original participants showed that the kids (now all grown up) that had been good at deferring gratification had more prefrontal cortex (new brain) activity while the rest had more old brain activity. In other words, the early ability to activate, master and concentrate on using your new brain leads to being able to defer reward now in return for a greater reward at a later time. If your kids want to become astronauts, world class pianists, brilliant authors or brain surgeons this may be the single most important thing you can teach them.

Interestingly, there is a close correlation between trust and the ability to defer gratification. Prior to repeating the marshmallow test, a University of Rochester study made promises to two groups of children. One group had the promise broken; the other had it fulfilled. The children that had a promise broken prior to the marshmallow test had a much harder time deferring gratification than the children that had been promised something that they actually received prior to the marshmallow test.

This is interesting because it may mean that self-control is influenced both by analytical thinking *and* trust.

It is worth noting that a more recent study[18] questioned the findings in the original marshmallow study and argues that the capacity to hold out for a second marshmallow is shaped largely by a child's social and economic background. In this explanation model, it is the child's socioeconomic background that predicates the ability to delay gratification and increases chances of long-term success. Either way, there is no doubt that positive outcomes are strongly correlated to long-term planning and that the ability to stay on course and delay short-term gratification until the goal has been achieved is important, no matter what shapes it.

This is much in line with current neuroscience, which has shown our brain to be predictive, not reactive.[19] We now know that all our neurons are firing constantly, stimulating one another at various rates. This intrinsic brain activity has been among the greatest recent discoveries in neuroscience, but what is even more compelling is what this brain activity represents: millions of predictions of what you will encounter next in the world, based on your lifetime of past experience.

What We Actually *Do* Know about Impulse Control—And About Losing It!

In an article in the *Harvard Business Review*, researchers Kai Chi et al. analyzed 120 management papers related to self-control and found three main reasons underlying the *loss* of self-control in a given episode:

> Self-control is a finite cognitive resource; different types of self-control tap the same pool of self-control resources; and exerting self-control can negatively affect future self-control if it is not replenished. Think of self-control as analogous to physical strength: Our physical strength is limited, various tasks (e.g., football, basketball, walking, etc.) deplete it, and continued exertion can negatively affect future physical strength if it's not restored.[20]

It turns out that our power and control over our consciously chosen actions are quite fragile and easily used up. This, of course, is consistent with the fact that every part of our brain is dependent on basic biological needs to work properly. You will buy more food when shopping on an empty stomach. And you will make poorer decisions if you are angry or sleep-deprived. This carries some serious implications. Sufficient rest and nourishment are necessary for good decision-making, for one. And complicated decisions are best made earlier in the day than later, when your supply of self-control is more likely to be depleted.[21]

The U.S.-based Auto Insurance Centre, an insurance industry news and information site, did a study of how and when the hashtag #ROADRAGE was posted on Instagram.

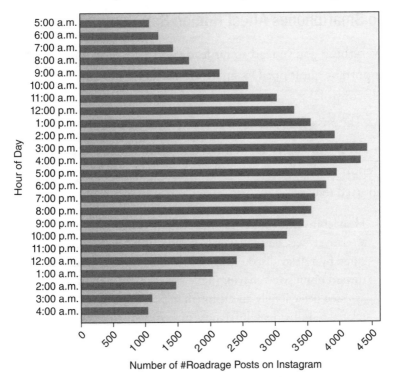

Number of #Roadrage Posts on Instagram

What they found was that road rage builds up during the day and over the week. Morning rush hour was found to be less prone to road rage than afternoon rush hour. And the later in the work week, the worse it gets, with Friday afternoon rush hour being the absolute peak of road rage. This seems to tally with the *Harvard Business Review* assessment on impulse control: when you combine a stressful situation (rush hour) with a situation where your impulse control is already low (after work), irrational and impulsive behavior soon follows. It was also telling that road rage postings peaked in the heat of July and August and were generally higher in cities with massive traffic and frequent gridlocks during rush hour.

Do Smartphones Affect Human Self-Control?

Everything you've read so far leads up to a logical and important question: Do smartphones affect human self-control?

The answer is yes!

In 2016, Henry H. Wilmer and Jason M. Chein published a report in the *Psychonomic Bulletin & Review*, where they reported that

> Heavier investment in mobile devices is correlated with a relatively weaker tendency to delay gratification (as measured by a delay discounting task) and a greater inclination toward impulsive behavior (i.e., weaker impulse control, assessed behaviorally and through self-report) but is not related to individual differences in sensitivity to reward.[22]

The study is based on a meta-analysis of research on impulse control, combined with new studies in which students' impulse control was measured before, during and after smartphone use. A similar study from the University of Bern comes to the same conclusion:

> People with lower self-control found it significantly harder not to react to the smartphone signal immediately. This effect remained stable, even when a series of further

personality features were also incorporated into the statistical model.[23]

Furthermore, a recent Korean study shows that smartphone addiction may be indirectly linked to commitment phobia.[24]

> The study of 376 Korean university students found that avoidant attachment was indirectly linked to smartphone addiction. People with higher levels of avoidant attachment [fear of relationships] tended to have lower self-esteem and more anxiety, which in turn was associated with smartphone addiction.[25]

In other words, if you have a hard time committing (which requires impulse control) your risk of smartphone addiction is higher. In essence these studies imply that we might all be in the midst of a global digital marshmallow test—but one that we seem to be losing, because these marshmallows merely consist of 1s and 0s; there's an endless supply of them, and they're your reward for *not* deferring gratification. They're made for the sole purpose of making us eat them—again and again, reinforcing our inability to defer gratification and greatly diminishing our ability to focus on things that matter, such as learning to play the violin, becoming a surgeon, or even being able to listen attentively to our loved ones.

Notes

1. Dopamine is actually a neurotransmitter and not a hormone—but the press keeps referring to it as a hormone.

2. http://science.sciencemag.org/content/275/5306/1593.full

3. Monoaminergic modulation of emotional impact in the inferomedial prefrontal cortex. Geday, Jacob; Gjedde, Albert. In: *Synapse*, Vol. 63, No. 2, 2009, pp. 160–6.

4. https://www.scientificamerican.com/article/how-the-brain-gets-addicted-to-gambling/

5. http://www.jneurosci.org/content/30/18/6180.full

6. https://www.theguardian.com/science/2013/feb/03/dopamine-the-unsexy-truth

7. https://www.billboard.com/articles/list/2155531/the-hot-100-all-time-top-songs?list_page=7

8. https://www.ncbi.nlm.nih.gov/pmc/articles/PMC3936960/pdf/nihms555317.pdf

9. http://www.adultdevelopmentstudy.org/grantandglueckstudy

10. https://www.ncbi.nlm.nih.gov/pmc/articles/PMC4286383/

11. https://www.ncbi.nlm.nih.gov/pubmed/24115941

12. https://ifstudies.org/blog/technoference-in-parenting-is-your-mobile-device-distracting-you-from-your-child

13. Hiniker, A., Sobel, K., Suh, H., Sung, Y. C., Lee, C. P., & Kientz, J. A. (2015, April). Texting while parenting: How adults use mobile phones while caring for children at the playground. In *Proceedings of the 33rd annual ACM conference on human factors in computing systems* (pp. 727–736).

14. Ibid.

15. Ibid.

16. https://hbr.org/2016/11/have-we-been-thinking-about-willpower-he-wrong-way-for-30-years

17. https://en.wikipedia.org/wiki/Stanford_marshmallow_experiment

18. https://www.theatlantic.com/family/archive/2018/06/marshmallow-test/561779/

19. https://www.edge.org/annual-question/2016/response/26707

20. *Harvard Business Review*: Leadership Takes Self-Control. Here's What We Know About It by Kai Chi (Sam) Yam, D. Lance Ferris and Douglas Brown. https://hbr.org/2017/06/leadership-takes-self-control-heres-what-we-know-about-it

21. https://pdfs.semanticscholar.org/b8e5/ebf19b927c67a341aff9e
    c5635789672ecdf.pdf

22. https://link.springer.com/article/10.3758/s13423-016-1011-z

23. http://www.unibe.ch/news/media_news/media_relations_e/
    media_releases/2018/medienmitteilungen_2018/low_self_control_
    influences_smartphone_use/index_eng.html

24. http://www.unibe.ch/news/media_news/media_relations_e/
    media_releases/2018/medienmitteilungen_2018/low_self_control_
    influences_smartphone_use/index_eng.html

25. https://www.psypost.org/2018/04/smartphone-addiction-
    indirectly-linked-commitment-phobia-according-new-psychology-
    research-51120?utm_source=TrendMD&utm_medium=cpc&utm_
    campaign=PsyPost_TrendMD_0

Chapter Four

When the first iPhone hit the U.S. stores on 9 June 2007, it cost $500. Yet six million units were sold before the next model arrived. Eight years later, in 2015, a total of 1.4 *billion* smartphones were in the hands of users scattered across the globe.[1] That same year, the *Journal of Computer Mediated Communication*[2] published a study in which a group of iPhone users were asked to complete word puzzles. During the exercise, research assistants called their personal phones at erratic intervals and for a varying number of rings; the users could hear their phones ring but were prevented from answering. The objective was to measure whether and to what extent anxiety levels were triggered when someone is blocked from answering a ringing phone.

Not surprisingly, this frustrating exercise caused an increase in heart rate and blood pressure for most of the subjects. They also reported unpleasant feelings, including anxiety. These results may seem predictable; who wouldn't be annoyed in the above scenario? But the study embedded another measure into the test that helps explain *why* we feel iPhone separation anxiety. The researchers inquired about the subjects' sense of "extended self," a concept that dictates that humans' overreliance on a given object ultimately leads us to identify the object as an extension of ourselves, in this case the iPhone. So, if you're cut off from your iPhone, it's on a psychological continuum with, say, having one of your fingers cut off (although not overtly physically painful). Interestingly, in 2015, the experiment centered exclusively on phone calls. Obviously if the same experiment were done today, the paradigm would shift from phone calls to notifications and other alerts that are signaled by a visual effect, a buzz or other sounds.

Is this any different from previous changes in society like television, radio, pop music or even comic books? We would argue that yes, what we experience here is different and not least because we are seeing it on a much larger scale than ever before. As we've discussed, smartphones have been adapted more quickly and more widely than any other technological advance in history. This means they reached critical cultural mass before a pilot group of users could report some preliminary indications of negative (or positive) effects—as the law would have required in the case of the pharmaceutical or automotive industry. In the twentieth century, television and radio experienced a rapid adoption after an initial seeding, but these devices were both immobile and passive, two qualities that limited their diffusion throughout daily life. (Those who remember early cordless phones may recall feeling rather dizzy at the prospect of being able to walk around the house while talking to your friends—it was *that* radical.) This all changed with the arrival of the smartphone and subsequently tablets. These devices could be carried around, touched, looked at and listened to at all times, and this laid the foundation for the most powerful human-to-gizmo mind–body meld ever seen in history. Through this development—and probably based on a gradually more and more extended "iSelf,"—smartphones like the iPhone have slowly become no longer just a device, but a digital DNA chart of you, your interests and—most importantly—what captures your attention a large percentage of your time.

The Human Information Factory

A 2015 report by Microsoft Canada stated that the human attention span had now dropped to merely eight seconds—that's one second less than that of a goldfish. This claim made headlines all over the world.[3,4,5] Fortunately, however, this statistic was a total fabrication that was soon debunked—although by then it had already spread around the globe like wildfire. The incident is worth noting because although not true, the average person found it perfectly believable based on their own observations of life in the digital age.[6,7] And even if the goldfish story didn't hold water, it's believable for a reason: our brains are indeed *that* vulnerable.

The Limited Working Memory

Look at this picture for a few seconds. (Have a paper and pen ready.)

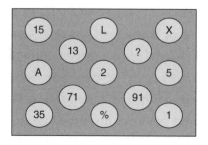

Now look elsewhere and write as many of the figures as
you can on a piece of paper. Chances are good that you'll only
remember 5–7 out of the 13 possible symbols. We owe this
lousy batting average to our brain's meagre working memory
capacity. Like a relay station, working memory temporarily
holds information for further processing.[8] What this means
in today's world is that your working memory is not just
continually full but chronically backed up. It also means
that it *never* gets to rest. We don't yet know the long-term
consequences of this added burden placed on brain function.
Requiring additional resources means they must be drawn
from *somewhere* … but at what price to the brain's long-term
overall function? Stay tuned ….

The Sorting Task

Another important human frailty is our limited ability to
filter the onslaught of information. Consider for a moment
how you experience the world around you. You look at it,
you feel it, you hear it, you smell it or you taste it. But how
much information does the brain actually receive through the
senses—and how much of that information is *actually* needed?
Neuroscientist Manfred Zimmermann has estimated that our
total capacity for perceiving or taking in information through
our sensorium is about 11 million bits per second.[9] And,
as you recall, most of this information—almost 10 million
bits per second—reaches our brain through our eyes, with
the rest being transferred mostly from our hearing and lastly
from the three remaining senses. However, only 40 bits (out
of 10 million) is useful—according to your subconscious
filter, anyway. And that just happens to be the amount of

information that surfaces to consciousness. The question is, then, just how good is the brain's filter at separating the good bits from the useless ones? Is it really letting the important stuff through the autopilot and into your conscious thought?

Information Processing

Our sense organs transform external stimuli into electrochemical signals that travel along nerve pathways to our brain. The brain in turn memorizes and stores the information for long-term access. But how does all of this happen? Let's imagine that a certain bundle of signals has reached your brain—for example, let's say you're walking past a rose garden. Before the brain can register the scent and image as "roses," it must run an elaborate processing and translation task. First, it must actively select the most important "channel" to focus attention on, in this case your nose. But this requires a trade-off, and it must at the same time deselect or become defocused to irrelevant signals from other sensory channels. Imagine you are reading a book when construction noise starts up outside. Your first move will probably be to look up to scan your surroundings for a threat (we've been wired like that since prehistoric times). Seeing no threat, you return to your book. In essence, what you just did was shift between channels, something we do all the time without being particularly conscious of these shifts. Once a channel is selected, rough processing begins and the brain delegates responsibility for finer processing to the appropriate components.

This occurs through a process called "encoding." Encoding enables the brain to match incoming signals to previous experiences that may indicate appropriate responses based on past events. If there's no direct match, your brain moves on to the next best thing, namely, assumptions or even prejudices associated with a given piece of information. This encoding phase of information processing is probably the most crucial one in the chain because it has such a big impact on our understanding and perception of the world. Finally, all of the recently connected dots are stored in your short-term memory,[10] momentarily making it possible for you to recall it. And power of recall is obviously essential if you're going to access the previously digested information as a basis for the appropriate response to a stimulus, whether it's a meaningful reply to a question, or stepping on your brake pedal when you see a red light.

Think of the various stations that information must pass through on its way to consciousness—where it can stimulate *action*—as train tracks. Now you can easily see the junctures at which those mythical train robbers can hold up the mail and switch letters from your loved ones for their own product pitches. And today's marketers know that the brain is most vulnerable when overloaded. This is also why the idea that you can multitask *with the same part of the brain* is a myth. You can, of course, drink water and listen to music at the same time, but the moment you try to listen to two people simultaneously, things start falling apart; your cognitive processing can only do one thing at a time and trying to multitask comes at the cost of misinterpreting, missing or failing to properly store incoming signals.

In this way, you can see how the smartphone could be viewed as a "weapon of mass distraction." And it seems that few of us have any real idea how attached we are to our devices. A 2015 British study carried out by a group of psychologists

showed two surprising facts: (1) that young adults used
their phones an average of five hours a day, and 2) that the
actual use was in fact roughly *twice* as much as they estimated
themselves, indicating behavior that is automatic to the point
of being below the threshold of consciousness. "This suggests
that we urgently need to research into the psychodynam-
ics of these technologies, in terms of the emotional—and
possibly psychopathological—function they are serving
in people's lives,"[11] remarked the British psychologist
Richard House, who researches the impact of technology on
human experience.

Would You Dare to Be a Passenger in a Car Driven by a Distracted You?

In 2012, the U.S. National Safety Council released a white
paper entitled "Understanding the distracted brain—why
driving using hands-free cell is risky behavior."[12] Using the
information processing model mentioned above, the white
paper made the case that distracted driving is just as bad as
speeding or drunk driving. The Council argued that while
most "hands-free" devices do indeed help drivers keep their
hands on the wheel and eyes on the road they do not elim-
inate "cognitive distraction," which is the term for a driver
"taking his mind off the road." Researchers have identified
a phenomenon known as "reaction-time switching costs,"[13]
and have found that talking on your cell phone while driving,
even if the phone is hands-free, increases your reaction time.
What this really implies is when the brain is overloaded with
information, it starts missing beats. And this has a critical
impact on our ability to react appropriately. The report

also concludes that we probably haven't even scratched the surface in terms of understanding the relationship between subconscious cognitive distraction and accidents.

Excuse Me, Do You Have a Minute?

Driving a car is one thing, but how does distraction manifest in a broader field of activity, such as the workplace? A 2013 Michigan State University study asked participants to perform a sequence-based task on a computer to simulate office work. Researchers found that three-second interruptions doubled the error rate and four-and-a-half second interruptions *tripled* the number of errors. Why did the error rate spike up so dramatically? As lead researcher Dr. Erik Altmann observed: "The answer is that the participants had to shift their attention from one task to another. Even momentary interruptions can seem jarring when they occur during a process that takes considerable thought."[14] But that's not all. University of California Irvine researchers shadowed workers on the job, studying their productivity.[15] They found that even after a distraction has subsided and a person is mentally ready to get back on track, there's a time-lag you need to overcome first. The same results of distractions being connected to increased error rates were also found in an Australian study where nurses were observed while they prepared and administered a total of 4271 medications to 720 patients in Australian hospitals. The researchers concluded that each interruption resulted in a 12.7% increased risk of a medication error and that the error rate tripled when nurses were interrupted six or more times while doing their tasks.[16]

Smartphones and Feelings

In many respects, using your smartphone while driving is
like driving slightly drunk. You feel okay, but you are actually
slower to respond to critical situations. And that is not all.
People with unhealthy digital habits may well find themselves
using their smartphone rather like alcohol—as a way to manage feelings. In her doctoral thesis[17] British sociologist Jane
Vincent demonstrated how we use the cellphone to mediate
emotions and how this colors our perceptions. She found that:

> Within this group of respondents, the mobile phone not
> only had become a key component in their daily emotional
> management of their everyday lives, but also that mobile
> phone use had a profound effect on sense of self. In this
> context, mobile phones are used extensively to manage the
> presentation of self, as well as the emotional highs and lows
> of relationships and family commitments.[18]

In other words, people now seem to use their smartphones
to also manage more complex things such as relationships and
emotional issues. Thus, it has evolved far beyond its original
station as a practical tool: "It is also a repository of the emotional memories with which respondents interact."[19]

Research psychologist Larry Rosen has spent 30 years
studying the impact of technology on 50 000 children, teens
and adults in the United States and 24 other countries.
He concludes that connecting virtually is not the same as
real-world bonding:

> Our real and virtual worlds certainly overlap, as many of
> our virtual friends are also our real friends. But the time and
> effort we put into our virtual worlds limit the time to

connect and especially to communicate on a deeper level in our real world. With smartphone in hand, we face a constant barrage of alerts, notifications, vibrations and beeps warning us that something seemingly important has happened and we must pay attention.[20]

Jean Twenge is another researcher who has also spent years uncovering the impact of technology on humans. In an article in *The Atlantic,* she concluded:

> The arrival of the smartphone has radically changed every aspect of teenagers' lives, from the nature of their social interactions to their mental health. These changes have affected young people in every corner of the nation and in every type of household. The trends appear among teens poor and rich; of every ethnic background; in cities, suburbs, and small towns. Where there are cell towers, there are teens living their lives on their smartphone.[21]

A Quick Pit-Stop Before Heading into the Land of Dragons

In the next couple of chapters, we will take you on a journey into the world of addictive software design, mind hacks, micro-segmentation, remarketing and retargeting, shopping cart abandonment reactivation, FOMO (Fear Of Missing Out) approaches, scarcity approaches, orchestrated tribalism, cognitive bias, and more. We think you will be surprised to see the level of digital manipulation that is being used against you—and having read the preceding chapters you now have the knowledge you need to understand what sort of biological and psychological mechanisms these approaches are hacking and reorchestrating to capture your attention and keep it captured for as long as they can.

But before we do so let's just take a moment to recap the highlights of what you have read so far.

1. The use of smartphones and social media is sweeping the world at an unbelievable pace. Two-thirds of the global population has access to smartphones and nearly half of the global population uses social media of some sort.

2. Tech Titans such as Google, Apple and Facebook are at the forefront of an industry that is as large as the total economy of many countries. Most of the players in this economy are engaged in a battle for your attention.

3. Your attention has become a global commodity being sold to advertisers that want to sell you goods, services, entertainment and so on.

4. Around 70 000 years ago something happened to kick-off an extraordinary change in the human species—our potential to think, share, analyze, create and imagine all came together to create the animal we are now. An animal that sits at the top of the food chain, dominates the world and has, for all practical purposes, won the evolutionary race against all other species.

5. You and your brain are in large part the result of an evolutionary development that has provided your forebears with a set of tools and routines that allowed you to become a social animal. You are by nature good at interacting with others, reading their emotions, building trust and having empathy for their plight. You even have hormones that help regulate social interaction and promote bonding and togetherness.

6. Your brain, and with it your consciousness and your ability to be attentive, is a "work in progress." The parts of your brain that manage autonomous functions and emotional reactions and responses are relatively old. The parts of your brain that let you learn things, solve problems, speak and do mathematics are fairly new. The two systems are connected and work together on many different levels to allow you to function and to think and to be.

7. Your cognitive processes operate in one of two different modes: slow or fast (conscious reasoning or autopilot). The slow mode requires a large amount of energy to run but allows you to reason, to figure things out and to learn new skills. The fast mode is impulsive and operates mainly on the basis of subconscious processing of past experience. It takes effort to engage the slow mode while the fast mode can be triggered easily by any number of factors.

8. As the newer parts of your brain evolved to allow you to tackle more complex tasks there was a need to mediate and move information back and forth between the old and the new system. This mediator is what we now call "consciousness" and the self-awareness you feel may simply be an unintentional side effect of the need for mediation between cognitive processes. Some scientists argue that this self-awareness while having a biological foundation cannot be described just as biology but must be considered a thing in-and-of itself.[22]

9. The consciousness you are experiencing (or think you are experiencing) is in reality a fragile and fairly strange construct. Parts of your perception of reality appear to

be time-shifted by about half a second to allow the older and the newer parts of your brain to operate in sync. And contrary to the popular idea of consciousness as being some sort of agent of volition and free will, your consciousness may to a large extent simply be a framework designed to mediate cognitive processes in which there is no "real consciousness" as you probably understand it, when you think about yourself. However, it's also possible that while consciousness may be the result of a number of subconscious processes it can still be shaped by itself and therefore we do have free will and volition.

10. There are "cracks" in our armor that allow outside distractions to engage internal cognitive processes in ways that are not part of the original set of stimuli our brain was designed for. It would appear that we tend to think of and respond to tools we use often (like smartphones) as part of our body and there are many studies to show that being distracted by technology has associated costs in "real life." Among the primary issues identified are "technoference," the consequences of attention that should have been placed in a specific task or relation (such as child-rearing) being co-opted by technology. Another issue is "switching costs"—the fact that shifting attention back and forth between systems or between your phone and the real world has costs in terms of precision, ability to concentrate and how quickly you can respond appropriately to danger.

So there you have it: you and your brain are a marvelous, but also somewhat fragile, construction that uses a large number of surprisingly strange processes to function—many of which are subconscious and take place without your self-aware consciousness knowing about or being able to interfere with them. You are a very bright, flexible construct designed to think and reason on your own as well as to interact and engage with others to build relationships, tribes and societies and so on—but at the same time this wonderful construction also has some serious flaws that can be exploited by external triggers. Flaws, that allow particular types of interaction design, storytelling, triggers and so forth to "break into" the space between your conscious self and your subconscious autonomous systems and which can be used to manipulate, seduce and coerce you into exhibiting behaviors that make profits for tech companies, but which may not be all that good for you.

Exactly how that works is what the next couple of chapters are about.

Notes

1. https://www.statista.com/statistics/266219/global-smartphone-sales-since-1st-quarter-2009-by-operating-system/

2. https://academic.oup.com/jcmc/article/20/2/119/4067530

3. http://time.com/3858309/attention-spans-goldfish/

4. http://www.telegraph.co.uk/science/2016/03/12/humans-have-shorter-attention-span-than-goldfish-thanks-to-smart/

5. https://www.nytimes.com/2016/01/22/opinion/the-eight-second-attention-span.html?_r=3

6. https://www.bbc.com/news/health-38896790

7. https://business.linkedin.com/marketing-solutions/blog/best-practices--content-marketing/2016/the-great-goldfish-attention-span-myth--and-why-its-killing-cont

8. Miyake, A. and Shah, P. (eds.) (1999). *Models of working memory. Mechanisms of active maintenance and executive control.* Cambridge University Press.

9. Manfred Zimmermann. "Neurophysiology of Sensory Systems" in Robert F. Schmidt (ed.), *Fundamentals of Sensory Physiology*, New York, Springer (1986), p. 116

10. https://en.wikipedia.org/wiki/Short-term_memory

11. https://www.huffingtonpost.co.uk/entry/smartphone-usage-estimates_us_5637687de4b063179912dc96

12. https://www.nsc.org/Portals/0/Documents/DistractedDriving Documents/Cognitive-Distraction-White-Paper.pdf

13. https://www.nsc.org/Portals/0/Documents/DistractedDriving Documents/Cognitive-Distraction-White-Paper.pdf

14. https://www.cbsnews.com/news/study-3-second-distractions-double-workplace-errors/

15. https://www.ics.uci.edu/~gmark/chi08-mark.pdf

16. http://www.ncbi.nlm.nih.gov/pubmed/20421552

17. http://epubs.surrey.ac.uk/770244/1/Vincent_2011.pdf

18. http://epubs.surrey.ac.uk/770244/1/Vincent_2011.pdf

19. http://epubs.surrey.ac.uk/770244/1/Vincent_2011.pdf

20. Rosen, L. (2015). Yes: Connecting virtually isn't like real-world bonding. Pew Research, May 10. https://d3jc3ahdjad7x7.cloudfront.net/0M5hYm9ALYnPgtK3CfFWENr80ci6Pad4AvHaoqzxILQvPvjq.pdf

21. https://www.theatlantic.com/magazine/archive/2017/09/has-the-smartphone-destroyed-a-generation/534198/

22. https://www.britannica.com/topic/noumenon#ref182175

Chapter Five

One Great Big Online Market

Smartphones, the Internet and social media function in many ways like a classic bazaar, where goods, services and experiences of all sorts are for sale and where eager hawkers will do everything they can to get your attention. But unlike the classic bazaar, internet hawkers are automated, fiercely smart and relentlessly focused. It's a trillion-dollar market populated by behemoth whales (Apple, Google, Facebook, Amazon) as well as thousands of smaller fish like Netflix, Instagram, Twitter, Snapchat, Rentalcars.com, Expedia, Orbitz, Walmart, eBay, Target, Best Buy, Etsy, MoMondo, Ryanair, and Delta, to mention just a few.

All of these sites share a common interest—knowing what you want, grabbing your attention as quickly and cheaply as possible and getting you to make the transaction. They also know that success lies in preaching to the choir—they're not interested in expending resources in trying to sell you a guitar if you don't like guitars to begin with. To attract relevant attention at a reasonable cost, the marketers behind search engines, social media and the Internet have developed a wide range of tools to analyze and understand your propensities and interests. They find their targets based on what can be measured and understood about how you use the Internet.

The complexity and level of sophistication of these tools comes as a surprise to most people but we are under much closer scrutiny than is generally known. The fact is that we are all being targeted by the top brains in behavioral science and digital code, and they know how to match your information to the advertisers that are out to sell you goods, services and entertainment.

B.J. Fogg and the Stanford Persuasion Lab

In 1997, a Stanford PhD by the name of B.J. Fogg posed a very interesting question at a conference in Atlanta. After researching how people interact with computers, he realized that students gravitated toward computers that they had gotten good results from, even though objectively speaking, all of the computers functioned identically. Could it be, he wondered, that people relate to computers just as they would with other people?

This simple idea would have wide-ranging implications. Fogg's simple attempt to create better software for students eventually became known as the "Fogg Behavior Model," and ended up as the weapon of choice for anyone who wants to hypnotize you online with anything from a sales pitch to a political agenda. As Ian Leslie of *The Economist* puts it:

> Fogg called for a new field, sitting at the intersection of computer science and psychology, and proposed a name for it: "captology" (Computers as Persuasive Technologies). Captology later became behaviour design, which is now embedded into the invisible operating system of our

everyday lives. The emails that induce you to buy right away, the apps and games that rivet your attention, the online forms that nudge you towards one decision over another: all are designed to hack the human brain and capitalise on its instincts, quirks and flaws. The techniques they use are often crude and blatantly manipulative, but they are getting steadily more refined, and, as they do so, less noticeable.[1]

In essence, Fogg's Behavior Model says that three conditions are necessary to persuade you to take an action, such as making a purchase or clicking the "like" button:

1. You must want to do it.
2. You must be able to do it.
3. You must be triggered to do it.

Fogg showed that triggers only work when people are already highly motivated ("I really need a new sweater!") and when following through is easy (like the one-click checkout on Amazon). If the task is hard, you get frustrated and give up. Without sufficient motivation or ability, there's not enough force to carry you through the task if you meet resistance. And finally, there must be a stimulus.

Fogg had unintentionally found a surefire formula for keeping a user's eye on the ball: Offer them something they want, make it easy for them to get or use it, and continuously create triggers that keep them engaged.

The Fogg Behavior Model shows that three elements must converge at a given moment for a behavior to occur: Motivation, Ability, and Trigger. When a behavior does not occur, at least one of those three elements is missing.[2]

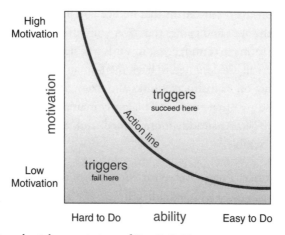

Reproduced with permission of Dr. B.J. Fogg.

Fogg himself added that the model "shows that motivation and ability can be traded off (e.g., if motivation is very high, ability can be low)" and that it "applies most directly to practical issues of designing for behavior change using today's technology."[3]

Let's Take a Look at B.J. Fogg's Model as It Is Being Used Today ...

On the following page is a typical Facebook page (belonging to one of the authors). You can observe a lot of B.J. Fogg-based design here. It is also well worth remembering (we will get into this in more depth later) that when you browse on the web the different sites you visit set "cookies" on your PC or phone so they can recognize you and your interests later. Let's take a look at what we see on this Facebook page.

- The blue top bar shows a profile picture to remind the user that this page is "you" (you identify the page as part of "you").

- The notification flags at the top provide a small dopamine reaction tempting me to discover who wants to friend me or what new notifications I have. These are "triggers," or actions I am motivated to perform *and* know how to perform!

- The advertisement for shoes is a piece of "remarketing"— A cookie tracked my recent shoe purchase and is now *re*marketing shoes to me through a profiling setup. Although the tracker has discovered that I was looking for shoes, it has not figured out that I already bought shoes or perhaps the segmentation model used believes my propensity for buying more shoes will be higher now that I've bought the first pair.

- The so-called "sponsored content" ends up in my feed for the same reason as the shoes: I have been looking for a new tablet and this activity has been captured with a cookie. The targeting probably also reflects cookies that show I buy a lot of kindle books. And you can see that they have used the "friends like" feature that enables them to show names of my friends that have "liked" an ad for their product. This makes me more likely to click on the advert.

- The advert for "How APIs are transforming business" reflects that I have been researching software technology for a project I am involved in.

In other words, everything that is on this particular page is carefully targeted to one of your authors, based on what Facebook and the advertisers know about him and what sites he has visited in the past. Also worth noting is the language used by these adverts: "An Absolute Game Changer" is a hook designed to make you curious and pull you in. And yes, it may be a very fine tablet, but will it change the game? Doubtful. The tagline "The Custom-Made Shoe Experience" works a little better. It conveys the idea that you can pick up a pair of high-class custom-made shoes right here and now, which is a credible trigger, if you are motivated to buy new shoes. The advert for the API is the weakest of the bunch—its call to action is generic instead of specific and our guess would be that this particular ad did not perform well.

A couple of other observations: The notifications on the left side of the screen (pages feed, memories, games) are Fogg-based triggers designed to keep you investing time in Facebook instead of heading somewhere else. And so is one of the finest features and inventions of social media—"the

infinity scroll"—with a high success rate for keeping you
engaged long past your intended time allotment because you're
now hypnotized by the screen unspooling endlessly like a road
trip to nowhere. You just blow past a lot of posts, but others
cause you to pause and read, perhaps even leaving a comment.
In reality, you're being held captive by the same mechanism
used in slot machines: you are browsing towards anticipation
of reward (a payoff of three cherries, a post you would like
to interact with). However, because the reward is dispensed
unpredictably the dopamine keeps flowing and you remain
engaged with the feed for a longer period of time. This design
feature is also known as "stickiness" and is something every
tech player in the business reveres and aims for as the pinnacle
of efficient design.

Your Phone Is a Slot Machine!

Here's a screenshot from Soren's Android phone (a Samsung Galaxy S8+ in case you were wondering). It's running an operating system called Android which is designed and owned by Google and it has the usual overload of applications that somehow made it onto the phone by persuading the owner they had something worthwhile to offer. At the last count there were about 100 applications installed on the phone—of which perhaps 15 are being used frequently.

The most obvious stickiness-hooks on the screenshot are the notifications with numbers that pop-up on top of the app-icon. These let the user know that "something" has happened, and you better come check it out (the sooner the better). Other common hooks are the icon designs (they are all colorful and attention grabbing) and the notification bar at the top of the screen where certain apps have gained access. On top of that there are all the lock-screen notifications (those messages that show up on your lock screen)—typically email headers, message headers and so on.

The original idea of notifications was a good one—to notify you of something that might need your attention. However, software developers soon realized that notifications were just another way of interacting with the user and could be designed to increase engagement. As soon as this became apparent, the notification wars began! Before long, every app ever created was clamoring for access to your "notification center" and for access to your screen.

As you know from the previous chapters of this book all of these notifications have an impact on you. They are directed at your "autopilot" or the "fast, impulsive layers" of your brain and they work exactly like waving a red cloth in front of a bull (actually bulls are colorblind, did you know?). They trigger an urge which, along with a small amount of dopamine, makes you want to find out what you are being notified of, in the hope of a "reward" (something that you feel good about engaging with). And because the system is set up so the rewards are unpredictable the pull becomes much stronger than if you knew exactly what you were getting when you click on the app.

The Pew Research Center in Washington has been tracking social media since 2012. In a 2018 report on social media use[4] they conclude that roughly two-thirds of US adults are Facebook users and that about three-quarters of those users access Facebook daily.

Interestingly, 40 percent of surveyed users said they'd find it difficult to give up social media, compared to only 28 percent when asked the same question in 2014. Obviously, back then social media was not as much of a prerequisite for engaging socially—but by now social media has become a big enough part of enough people's lives that it becomes hard to give it up, not just because it is addictive, but also because when everyone else uses it as their primary form of communication, giving it up means giving up your ability (or at least limiting it) to communicate with your community.

Whatever the reason, it appears that social media sites' increased use of addictive design is working.

What Do the Companies Targeting You See?

Facebook and many other social media platforms deliver interfaces designed to keep you stuck to their pages. They then open up for adverts that are designed to grab your attention and get you to visit the advertiser's website online store (or landing page). Let's take a look at the Facebook Ads manager store, where advertisers purchase potential customers' attention. Let's build a campaign for the book you are reading right now, just to show you the extent of detailed targeting that is available to advertisers.

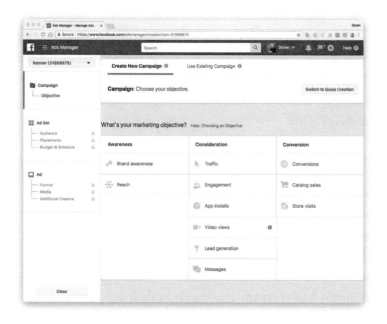

Imagine entering a supermarket and looking at a map of the different aisles. As you can see, this campaign can be programmed to target a specific audience and to run at strategic times. It can also be optimized to deliver on a specific set of goals, such as building brand awareness, getting users to download and install apps, generating leads for future sales or getting users to visit your online store and shop.

Here are some examples of how granular you can get in your audience selection.

First off, we've selected Cambridge, UK, as our target and
have narrowed our target audience to women between the ages
of 18 and 65. We can narrow our target group even further by
stipulating what sort of education we would like our targets
to have and we can also sort our groups based on interests or
behaviors such as going to concerts, eating Chinese food, or
going on hikes.

These days, you can target people by pretty much anything,
including whether or not you tend to shop online, what sort
of mobile phone you use, whether or not you like pets, yoga,
travel (and even what kind of travel). Users who've liked or
interacted with other Facebook pages are also targeted—so if
we find Facebook pages with lots of members and a theme
that's in alignment with buying this book, we can target them
directly.

But how on earth does Facebook know all this about you? Your interests, your education, your politics, your online behavior, your propensity for shopping? Simple: they collect and correlate every move you make on Facebook with that of other users. From an analytical standpoint you are part of a "cohort" with specific known traits. And if Facebook has solid knowledge that you fit four out of five data points in a given cohort the chances are good that you will fit the fifth as well. Is this way of generating profiling information on you perfect? No. But then again, it doesn't have to be. It just has to be good enough to allow the advertisers to reach you at a cost that still allows them to make money after their online marketing costs have been paid. All of this information about you is continuously collected by Facebook as you interact with it. These data profiles form the basis for the very accurate targeting that Facebook uses to sell about $50 billion-worth of adverts a year.

It's important to understand that in addition to being accurate, this profiling and targeting information is also flexible and continuously upgraded with new knowledge. Imagine that we posted an advert for this book, targeting 25 specific audience groups. Our first step, then, will likely be to monitor how those groups perform. Perhaps 15 of these groups like our offering and buy our book while the other 10 groups are less responsive. In this case, we obviously would quickly turn off the 10 unresponsive groups and instead create new groups based on audiences that look like the ones that are performing well (in Facebook parlance, this is known as "lookalike audiences").

This is a very nifty feature and it assures that your adverts get better and better at reaching the right audience, allowing you to sell lots of books. Even better (and a little scary as well) this entire process is easy to automate so you can let software programs optimize the targeting of your adverts. And, as it turns out, this software usually ends up doing a better job at targeting potential buyers than we humans can.

Your Personality Can Be Predicted with Great Accuracy

Michal Kosinski is a Stanford assistant professor who holds a PhD in Psychology from the University of Cambridge. During his time at Cambridge he and Cambridge psychologist David Stillwell developed the "MYPERSONALITY PROJECT." As we shall see, the idea was simple but the ramifications far-reaching.

Kosinski and his colleagues started out with a personality test based on the "Big 5" model of personality traits[5] developed by J.M. Digman and Lewis Goldberg in 1990. In essence, the Big 5 model says that your personality can be described as a combination of five different traits: Openness, Conscientiousness, Extraversion, Agreeableness and Neuroticism (also often known as OCEAN). The typical Big 5 survey consists of about 100 questions that are designed to get an idea of how open, conscientious, extrovert, agreeable and neurotic you are.[6] The Big 5 model is widely used, and many studies have been undertaken to determine differences in personalities between men and women, between people hailing from different cultures or from different socioeconomic backgrounds.

But Kosinsky and Stillwell took Big 5 in an entirely different direction. First, they asked volunteers (of which there were hundreds of thousands) to take an online survey scoring their personality profile.[7] They also asked the volunteers for access to their Facebook profile, so they could correlate the results of the personality study with the behavior (likes, postings, pictures, groups, etc.) of the volunteer on Facebook. Next, they started running calculations on all this data using some of the same cohort techniques described earlier in this chapter. Before long, the model was refined to where a mere peek at a Facebook profile would provide a very accurate assessment of the user's personality, interests, affiliations, gender, sexuality and so on.

In 2012, Kosinski demonstrated that access to just 68 likes of a user on Facebook would predict skin color (95% accuracy), sexual orientation (88% accuracy), democrat or republican (85% accuracy). And it didn't stop there—grinding away at the data it soon became clear that Facebook data would provide a very good idea about a person's intelligence, religious affiliation, alcohol and drug use or even whether someone's parents were divorced. Eventually Kosinski and his partners tuned their models to a level where access to a mere 70 likes would allow it to deduce more about you than your close friends know, 150 likes more than what your *parents* know about you, and 300 likes would give them more knowledge about you than your *partner* has.

The implications of this are more than a little bit sobering. By simply scanning your Facebook page and analyzing your pattern of likes, postings, photos and so forth, a piece of software can now predict your personality, your likes, your interests, your affinities and your behavior more accurately than your friends, your parents and even your life partner.

Scary? We think so. Interestingly, "on the day Kosinski published these findings he received two phone calls. One was the threat of a lawsuit and the other a job offer. Both were from Facebook."[8] Kosinski eventually completed his PhD and went on to become an assistant professor at Stanford but the ramifications of the work he had started would soon turn into a debacle of epic proportions involving whistleblowers, allegations of rigging the US presidential elections (as well as Brexit), hearings in the US Senate and much more.

The Cambridge Analytica Scandal

In 2013, a British behavioral research company called the SLC Group formed a new spinoff company called Cambridge Analytica. The company was partly owned by Robert Mercer, an American computer scientist, who was an early artificial intelligence developer. The purpose of Cambridge Analytica was to do political consulting based on data mining, data brokerage and data analysis.

As it would later turn out, Cambridge Analytica had somehow obtained data associated with more than 87 million Facebook profiles (maybe including yours, who knows?). How did this happen? Well, Kosinski's original survey was designed as a Facebook app that asked users for permission to access their entire network. The survey had 270 000 participants and by asking them for access to not only their own Facebook data but also the data of their friends, and friends of friends, Kosinski gained access to the data of 87 million Facebook users. Facebook has since closed this hole in their privacy management.

How Cambridge Analytica obtained this data is unclear.

However, once Cambridge Analytica had the key to these 87 million profiles they could start untangling an even bigger puzzle—in essence reverse-engineering the results of Kosinski by comparing what was known about this profiling data with other data that they could acquire from many different sources. Using many of the same techniques that Facebook uses to deliver "lookalike audiences" to advertisers, Cambridge Analytica set out to profile as large a portion of the US public as they possibly could—by their own claim, several hundred million people.

All of these profiles were entered into databases that were in turn used to design and drive communication approaches based on individual profiles. If Cambridge Analytica knew the issues occupying you or how you felt about them, then that was what they would write about as they kept focusing adverts and emails on you.

Many claims have been made that the Donald Trump campaign's use of Cambridge Analytica data to drive his campaign garnered him the presidential election. And as most will be aware, the aftermath of the revelation of how Cambridge Analytica misused 87 million Facebook profiles led to a senate hearing, to the bankruptcy of Cambridge Analytica, and to Facebook implementing new and much more strict privacy policies.

Did Cambridge Analytica in fact help Donald Trump win the election?

The authors of this book doubt it. As we shall see a little further down the road, profiling data is extremely handy when it comes to targeting customers and selling them goods and services, but it turns out that getting people to change their values and politics is much harder.

Either way, what we can learn from Kosinski's work on profiling is that once you have enough data on a fairly large group of people, then only very little data is needed to take a very good guess at how a given consumer will behave when presented with an offering, whether it's a product, a service or a group affiliation. And as you will soon see, that insight is being relentlessly used against you by both Facebook and Google, and the advertisers they service.

How You Are Captured and Converted

Obviously, for the thousands of marketers that use the major internet platforms to sell their goods and services, this is just the head of the trail. In order to sell to you, a few more things have to happen, and a lot of it is predicated on B.J. Fogg.

First, advertisers need to entice you temporarily away from Facebook (or Google) and get you into their own domain or shop. Making this work basically consists of several steps: displaying something that piques your interest and makes you click; providing a landing page for your click (the page you are directed to when you click on an advert) that is appealing, and which makes it easy for you to want to part ways with some of your money in return for whatever it is the vendor is selling.

Predictably, enticing you to learn more about a product or service by presenting it as efficiently as possible (from the advertisers' point of view) has given birth to an industry of its own. The picture on the next page is a screen grab from an online marketing platform called "Unbounce"—a company that specializes in templates for advertisers to build efficient landing pages that generate lots of sales. As you can see, Unbounce is brutally honest about its use of addictive design in their landing page templates. The goal: "drive more leads and revenue from any web page by showing targeted popups and sticky bars to specific users." Unbounce is in no way unique—there are many other companies out there supplying the same sort of service.

In essence, Unbounce helps its customers (advertisers) systemize and optimize their management of your attention. The graphic above describes the process and tools they offer. Behind the Unbounce template is a process and workflow that makes it easier for advertisers to build and test landing pages you can't resist clicking on. Your click converts your interest into sales by a number of mechanisms, including on-screen chatting, emails, remarketing if the sale fails, and a host of other functions. It's all completely automated, and because the software learns by doing, it constantly improves its ability to lasso you with attention-grabbing offers you can't refuse.

At this point you are probably beginning to get a sense of just how efficient the digital manipulation you are being exposed to is. If you find this worrying, just wait till you see just how deep this rabbit hole goes …

Multivariate Testing—Helping Consumers Capture Themselves

Let's assume for a moment—purely theoretical of course—that we have a really interesting book about the side effects of smartphones and social media we want to sell to you. We understand how we can use Facebook or Google to get your attention at a reasonable cost, and we know how to get you to click on an advert generated by one of these services. We also have a pretty good idea of who our core audience might be. But once a potential customer clicks on an advert and ends up on our landing page, marketers still must find the right message and the right look to maximize sales.

In the last century, advertising agencies hired copywriters and art directors to knock together adverts that they thought would have impact. In the early days, they worked on intuition and observation, and because they were experienced professionals they often got it right—but not as right as software can today.

Say hello to "multivariate testing,"[9] a very powerful way of letting consumers decide what works best for them. The basic idea is simple. Let's assume you want to build a landing page that sells this theoretical book really well. This landing page will typically consist of a number of elements: a headline, a couple of paragraphs about the book, a picture of the book, perhaps a picture of the authors, endorsements from readers, and so on. Nothing unusual about the recipe—if you buy and read books you have probably already seen some version of it a thousand times.

But imagine that you started out by deciding to test different ways of constructing your landing page in order to find the best-selling one. Let's say you create 10 headlines, 10 different descriptions of the book, 10 different photos, 10 different "calls to actions" and 10 different ways of organizing endorsements, plus you decide to do the layout of all this in 10 different designs (headline at the top, headline under the photo of the book, etc.).

This would be an interesting experiment if not for the fact that you would need to design and test 600 000 landing pages to find out which one was best.

Here's where multivariate testing comes into the picture—via a piece of software it automatically generates landing pages that matches your requirements—and it does not need to run tests on 600 000 pages to tell you which landing pages perform best—thanks to a very smart algorithm that manages to break your possible variates into a number of cells that are then optimized by analysis of how clicks (customers) respond to each cell. The best performing software in this category would only need about 5000 clicks to tell you with 99.9% accuracy which of your 600 000 test pages sell the most books!

And obviously once advertisers harness the power of user-testing on their landing page design (or in their online shop or anywhere else) they realize that the same approach can also be used to divide up audiences and sell more because they can target better and more precisely. This way advertisers can (and do) test their way to realizing that swimwear landing pages with pictures of bikinis sell better in California while one-piece swimwear sells better in the Midwest.

As you are probably beginning to realize, the adverts you see on your screen are designed to target you personally. When you click on them, the pages you reach have most likely been tested extensively and are predictive of your desires. But wait—there's more!

The Strange World of Tracking Pixels, Cookies and Remarketing

There are many different ways websites (such as Facebook and Google or advertiser sites such as Walmart or eBay) can keep track of your comings and goings. This is regardless of whether you access these sites via a smartphone, a tablet or a nice old-fashioned iMac (like the one this book was written on). As you browse the Internet many of the sites you visit leave "cookies" on your device—small files that collect data. Some of these cookies are "tracking cookies" (sometimes also known as third-party cookies) and as the name implies, these cookies track your browsing and they can be read by many different advertisers. These cookies send a log of your online activities to a remote database for analysis. Some cookies only collect and send anonymous information while others actually collect and send specific user information that can include names and addresses to the tracker host.

If you have been browsing online shops, social media and news sites for just a little while and stop to take a look at what your browser has picked up, you should not be surprised to discover several hundreds of these cookies stored in your browser and waiting to track your daily little burst of news, social media and/or dopamine. All of this data (and it is a lot) is collected and used by advertisers in a number of ways—ways that are becoming increasingly more sophisticated. When an advert is

about to be loaded to a page you are browsing, the host serving
the adverts (this is just another piece of automated software)
looks for cookies on your browser it can use to determine what
adverts to show and can also send a record of your visit to the
advertiser in order to make it possible to target you even more
precisely at your next visit. Some ads will even address you by
name and mention your location.

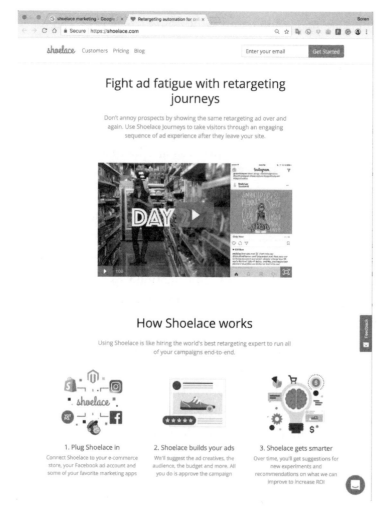

The illustration on the previous page is the homepage of a "retargeting" company called Shoelace. Their software enables advertisers to put a stream of adverts in front of you based on what they know about you (information collected via cookies, tracking pixels, IP addresses, and more). So let's say you have been spending some time on Facebook. And you got tracked browsing a group that sells books. Let's further assume I have 10 different books I would like to sell to you.

Shoelace makes it possible to show you my books on other pages you visit—and since I don't want to wear your attention out by showing you the same book over and over again (because that would lead to a lack of interest), I can keep trying to throw different titles at you to see what piques your interest. What's more, Shoelace is smart—it learns from experience. As it keeps track of how you respond, there's a snowball effect and its algorithms get to know you better and better. And that leads to ever more potent advertising.

So, in essence, you are being targeted with adverts based on deep knowledge of your interests, browsing habits, purchasing habits and so forth. And because of the continuous testing and optimization of approaches, content and design used by advertisers they get better and better at hitting their mark. Mind you—not everyone that clicks on a landing page buys a product or service and for most marketers a conversion rate (the percentage of clicks that convert to sales) of around 1–3% is just fine and more than enough to pay for the clicks that did not convert as well as leave a tidy profit.

From the advertiser's perspective this all makes sense. *Of course,* they're maximizing their advertising dollars. But from your perspective as a consumer, you are part of a precarious balance and you may not like your place in this ecosystem if you see what's really happening. It goes like this: The titans offering the eyeballs (Google, Facebook, etc.) are looking to make as much revenue as they can by keeping your attention riveted. The advertisers would like to purchase your attention as cheaply as possible in order for them to make more money. You are caught in the middle. As long as Google and Facebook can continue to grow their audiences, the balance between the need for revenue growth and delivering a good user experience can be met. At some point, however, when all of the users have been onboarded and the advertisers are paying as much as they can afford to pay while still being able to make money, then what?

It's hard to tell exactly how that dilemma will play out but given the fact that nearly half the world's population is already using these services (and by far the majority of citizens in the countries with the most developed economies) there is little doubt that the "showdown in Techistan" will be taking place sooner rather than later.[10]

All Aboard the Consumer Journey Train

If you are an entertainment provider, an e-retailer, an online bookshop or any other sort of potential advertiser, the latest trend in online marketing is the construction of complete customer journeys. Think of it as a complete set of rails laid out in front of you and designed to keep you engaged by exposing you to a number of different approaches.

Goal number one is getting you from Facebook or YouTube or Google to a landing page. But what happens if you do not respond to the offer on the landing page? Then there has to be some other trigger that can move you to the online store and get you browsing there.

Let's say you find something you like, and you put it in your "shopping cart." Let's back up for a sec—of course we mean your *online* shopping cart, which is a *very* different breed of cat than the cart you push around at the grocery. Just imagine, for example, that your shopping cart at Whole Foods prompted you to take certain actions *without you even realizing it.* That's what your online shopping cart is designed for! Just look at what happens if you go to checkout and then have second thoughts. You decide not to purchase that fake fur chinchilla hat after all and leave the site. Needless to say, that's anathema to all stations in this chain of commerce. That's "shopping cart abandonment" and that simply won't do. Luckily for the advertiser, his intelligent customer journey software (often also known as a marketing automation solution) takes care of things. It shoots off a quick email to let you know that it thinks you should come back and complete your purchase. And at the same time it waits and sees if it can catch you somewhere else—oh, hey, there you are browsing an article on a news site—and immediately delivers an advert or even better a "pop-up" window to that site informing you that your shopping cart is still there waiting for your purchase—with a 10 percent rebate but *only if you act now!*

You're probably starting to see that almost nothing you see online is random, generic or the same for everyone. It is high-precision marketing with a high definition scope that has you in its crosshairs and will plant its message literally inside the base of your skull, using numerous highly sophisticated ploys extracted from psychology and behavioral science.

The Horrible Dark Patterns

On top of all the tracking, the segmentation modeling, the testing, the retargeting and the "customer journeys" there are also a number of ploys that are even more insidious. Here are just a few of them—chances are you have seen many of them before but may not have reflected on what they are designed to do. If you go to the website darkpatterns.org you will get a lot more detail and examples of some of these approaches:

- Disguised Ads: Adverts disguised as other kinds of content or navigation, in order to get you to click on them.

- Confirm Shaming: Guilting users into opting into something. The option to decline is worded in such a way as to shame the user into compliance.

- Forced Continuity: When your free trial with a service comes to an end your credit card is charged without any warning.

- Hidden Costs: At the last step of the checkout process you discover that unexpected charges have appeared, e.g. delivery charges, tax, etc.

- Price Comparison Prevention: The advertiser makes it hard to compare the price of an item with another item, so you cannot make an informed decision.

- Privacy Zuckering: Being tricked into publicly sharing more information about yourself than you really intended to. Aptly named after Facebook CEO Mark Zuckerberg.

- Roach Motel: Design that makes it easy for you to get in but difficult to opt-out. Test: See if you can find the button that deactivates your Amazon account in less than 10 minutes, we dare you. ☺

- Sneak into Basket: Somewhere during your purchasing journey the site sneaks an additional item into your basket, often through the use of an opt-out radio button or checkbox on a prior page.

How Google Skews Your Search Results

If you are like most of us, Google is your "go-to" resource when it comes to searching of any kind. But did you know that the search results Google delivers are not generic but rather personalized to you and skewed by Google to fit their idea of what you would like to see?

There is not necessarily anything wrong with Google using the information they have on you to provide search results they think you would like—but there is a very real danger that it promotes "confirmation bias" in your engagement with the online world, causing you to believe fake news, rely on unreliable news sources and ultimately develop a distorted view of reality—if you don't look out. More on this later.

Let's take a look at some of the methods Google uses to personalize your search results.[11] Let's say you search for "coffee shop" —Google will consider the following when determining what search results to send back to you:

- Location (captured by IP-number or the GPS in your phone).
- Previous search and browsing history (where you have been).

- Stored social media profile (what your friends have to say).

- The device you are using (are you on the go or stationary).

- Other Google Products you use—for adding later personalization.

Based on these and a number of other and more esoteric factors, the Google Search Engine Ranking Algorithm whips up your personalized search results (and in fact does so 40 000 times per second or a staggering 3.5 billion times a day).

Now this is all good and fine when it helps Google help you find a coffee shop that serves extra hot soy milk (no fat), caffeine-free (skinny) cafe latte. But how about when you are searching to find news of the world around you? How do you feel about getting plugged into news sources, based not on a generalization but on specific profiling of you as a person? Or what about if you use Google to research an ethical dilemma, or the pros and cons of a particular political position? Are you still happy to have search results delivered based on profiling?

And obviously personalized search is not the only area where Google is skewing its search results. As many will be aware, the EU recently fined Google $2.7 billion[12] for skewing search results for shoppers to favor outlets that Google has an interest in or have received advertising revenue from.

Google has appealed the fine, claiming no wrongdoing: "While some comparison-shopping sites naturally want Google to show them more prominently, our data shows that people usually prefer links that take them directly to the products they want, not to websites where they have to repeat their searches," according to Kent Walker, Google SVP and general counsel.

However, a 2015 study undertaken by Harvard Business School professor Michael Luca and Columbia Law School professor Tim Wu finds that Google does indeed skew results. In their preamble, they say that "by prominently displaying Google content in response to search queries, Google is able to use its dominance in search to gain customers for this content. This may reduce consumer welfare if the internal content is inferior to organic search results."[13]

So, to recap—now you know just how much the tech industry and advertisers know about you and you have seen some of the techniques they use to keep you riveted to their services. In the next chapter we will take a look at what all this hoopla does to your cognitive apparatus.

Notes

1. https://www.1843magazine.com/features/the-scientists-who-make-apps-addictive

2. http://www.behaviormodel.org/

3. Ibid.

4. http://www.pewinternet.org/2018/03/01/social-media-use-in-2018/

5. https://onlinelibrary.wiley.com/doi/abs/10.1002/job.742—an excellent paper on Big 5 and how scoring here predicts workplace performance.

6. While Big 5 is not the same as the 16 personality types described by the Myers-Briggs personality test they have much in common. https://www.idrlabs.com/personality-types.php

7. You can take the same survey here. https://discovermyprofile.com/personality.html

8. https://motherboard.vice.com/en_us/article/mg9vvn/how-our-likes-helped-trump-win

9. https://www.optimizely.com/optimization-glossary/multivariate-testing/#

10. Actually, this showdown has already begun. Facebook shares plummeted 43% in the wake of the Cambridge Analytica scandal then began climbing again. However, the decision made by Facebook to become much better at guarding privacy and to police their network better against hate speech and fake news, along with a significant drop in user growth, meant delivering a forecast under market expectations leading to a sharp drop in shares. At the same time Twitter, in an attempt to clean up some of the many fake profiles they were suffering from, saw a drop in earnings due to the actual number of users being a good deal lower than originally reported leading to a drop of more than $5 billion in value.

11. https://www.link-assistant.com/news/personalized-search.html

12. https://www.adweek.com/digital/google-faces-2-7-billion-fine-from-eu-over-skewed-search-results/

13. https://www.slideshare.net/lutherlowe/wu-l

Chapter Six

S o, there you are, sitting in front of the screen or peering down into your smartphone. It's been a long day and you feel the need to unwind. You have already spent a couple of hours on social media throughout the day, but you just keep going. There's something nice about how easy it is. Uncomplicated and yet in many ways more satisfying than TV because you are a direct participant and you never know what's going to happen. Will someone like your comments? Will someone new try to friend you? Will you discover something new about a friend? Maybe there is a good quiz coming up or a video with kittens? In many ways it is just like participating in a very unpredictable soap opera. And while all of this is going on your brain keeps you slightly high on small doses of dopamine, which in turn leads your "autopilot" to continue browsing, selecting, responding, engaging, picking, scrolling … all of it somewhere in that gray area just barely below your attentive conscious radar. And every bit of it designed to get you into that state—because once you are in the zone you will keep hanging on for a long time and during that time you and your eyeballs and your attention are earning money for whatever social media you are using.

But what happens to you and your brain when you keep diving back into that zone over and over and over again?

Stress, Low Self-Esteem, Anxiety and Sleep Disturbances

In 2015, the Pew Research Center in Washington surveyed 1800 people about stress and their use of social media.[1] What they found is that some—but not all—people get more stressed the more they engage with social media. They also found the relationship between stress and social media use to be indirect. "It is the social uses of digital technologies, and the way they increase awareness of distressing events in others' lives that explains how the use of social media can result in users feeling more stress."[2]

Furthermore, the study found that women as a whole tend to report more stress than men and tend to be more aware of stressful events in the lives of their closest friends and family. And it would appear that awareness of the stressful events of others' lives (as is often shared on social media) is a significant contributor to people's own stress. These findings are supported by another study undertaken by *College Student Journal*. This study looked at use of social media in college graduates and found that users tended to spend an average of two-and-a-half hours a day on social media, with women tending to spend more time online than men and often reporting losing sleep because of social media. Many users reported feeling closer to Facebook friends than those friends seen daily in *real* life and many reported feelings of stress, cravings and (especially among women) negative self-body image.[3]

A study undertaken for the American Psychological Association examined whether frequent Facebook use is associated with lower self-esteem. The study found that people who use Facebook frequently tend to have lower self-esteem than less frequent users and that exposure to upward social comparisons on social media could lower self-esteem further.[4] In other words, many frequent Facebook users compare themselves unfavorably to the other profiles they engage with, resulting in lowered self-esteem. Likewise, researchers in an Austrian study found that users reported lower moods after using Facebook for 20 minutes than a control group who just browsed the internet.[5]

Another study published by the journal *Computers and Human Behavior* found that people who use many different social media platforms are more likely to suffer from anxiety than people who use fewer platforms.[6] And yet another study conducted by the University of Pittsburgh in 2017 found a demonstrable link between social media and sleep disturbances. Interestingly, it turned out that logging on often was a stronger predictor of sleep disturbances than being logged on for long periods of time. This supports the many studies that show a link between addictive design, dopamine release and restlessness. In all fairness, the Pittsburgh team also had to acknowledge that they had no way of being sure whether it was social media causing disturbed sleep or if the problem was that those with disturbed sleep tend to spend more time on social media platforms.[7]

There is little doubt that evidence is mounting in regard to these potential side-effects of extended social media use. And it seems clear that while not every user will experience every side-effect there is a correlation between the level of use and the propensity to experience adverse effects.

Smartphones and Social Media Can Lead to ADHD in Adolescents

A recent study published by researchers from UCLA, USC and Keck School of Medicine in the *Journal of the American Medical Association*[8] found that frequent use of social media leads to increased risk of ADHD. "In this longitudinal cohort survey study of adolescents aged 15 and 16 years at baseline and without symptoms of ADHD, there was a significant association between higher frequency of modern digital media use and subsequent symptoms of ADHD over a 24-month follow-up."

As is the case with many other studies into use of smartphones and social media the researchers have a hard time determining cause and effect. In other words, is it extensive use of social media that leads to increased risk of exhibiting ADHD symptoms, is it the ADHD symptoms that lead to extensive use of social media or is there some other factor at work?

Can Use of Social Media Be Addictive?

Can the use of social media be addictive? This is a really interesting question and the best answer to it is "probably," with the caveat that it depends on who you are and what you bring to the game. As we have seen in previous chapters, many social media sites use interaction techniques that are based on the same logic as casino slot machines—the setup of expectations with unpredictable rewards leading to a continuous dopamine-driven longing to see what's next (what's further down the scroll, behind the next notification, etc.).

Studies have shown that this sort of design can create dependencies in some gamblers. The International Gaming Research Unit at Nottingham Trent University in England published a meta-study on social media addiction some years back[9] comparing results from 43 other studies and came to the conclusion that "it may be plausible to speak specifically of "Facebook Addiction Disorder" … because addiction criteria, such as neglect of personal life, mental preoccupation, escapism, mood modifying experiences, tolerance and concealing the addictive behavior, appear to be present in some people who use [social networks] excessively."[10] Another study undertaken by Swansea University in Wales found that some people experience psychological (and to some minor extent physical) withdrawal symptoms if they stop using smartphones and social media.[11]

DSM-5 is the Diagnostic and Statistical Manual of Mental Disorders put out by the American Psychiatric Association. It is used widely not just in the United States but in many other countries as well. The latest revision of the DSM-5 now includes addictive disorders caused by behavior; for example, addiction to gambling or internet gaming. This inclusion, however, has been controversial as many researchers believe that behavioral addiction has not been proven to the point where it can be used as a mental disorder diagnosis. A paper[12] published in 2017 by the Society for the Study of Addiction with the title "How can we conceptualize behavioral addiction without pathologizing common behaviors" asks a very relevant question: If addiction can happen to some but not all via behaviors they exhibit is it relevant ascribing the addiction to the behavior? They believe the causes of addiction may be found elsewhere and are critical of the addition of online addiction to the DSM-5 manual.

We guess it would be fair to say that the jury is out on the question of just how addictive social media is, and not least on what makes it addictive to some but not to others. There are quite a few observable and demonstrable trends and many examples you can point to where people spend much time online with apparently diminishing returns and you can point to quite a few other unwanted effects in some users after massive doses of social media. But it remains unclear exactly what triggers addictive behavior in this realm (is it the medium itself, or something already inherent in the user?). And it also remains unclear if the cases of addiction reported have social media as their root cause.

However, what is really worrying is not so much the observation that a single study may claim links between social media and anxiety, sleep disorders, low self-esteem, ADHD or many other problems.

What is more worrying is that so many studies point to a wide spectrum of detrimental effects related to usage of social media.

When Addictive Design and Basic Human Social Traits Clash

We are most definitely not accusing smartphone manufacturers or social media companies of creating these problems on purpose—we see them mostly as unintended side effects that are beginning to manifest as the use of smartphones and social media becomes ever more prevalent.

There is, however, little or no doubt that these sites use "addictive design" on purpose and that they understand very well how and why it works. Sean Parker, a co-founder and the first CEO of Facebook blatantly admits that

> The thought process was all about, "How do we consume as much of your time and conscious attention as possible?" And that means that we need to sort of give you a little dopamine hit every once in a while, because someone liked or commented on a photo or a post or whatever, and that's going to get you to contribute more content, and that's going to get you more likes and comments. It's a social validation feedback loop. ... You're exploiting a vulnerability in human psychology.[13]

Parker's claim was backed up by Chamath Palihapitiya, a former vice-president for user growth at Facebook, who in late 2017 admitted to *The Guardian* newspaper that addictive design played a decisive role in the success of Facebook and that he now regrets the use of it:

> The short-term, dopamine-driven feedback loops that we have created are destroying how society works. No civil discourse, no cooperation; misinformation, mistruth, this is not about Russian ads. This is a global problem. It is eroding the core foundations of how people behave by and between each other.[14]

Interestingly, Facebook does not deny Palihapitiya's allegations but instead released a statement saying that

> When Chamath was at Facebook we were focused on building new social media experiences and growing Facebook around the world, Facebook was a very different company back then, and as we have grown, we have realized

how our responsibilities have grown too. We take our role very seriously and we are working hard to improve.

Now, let's take a closer look at some of the ways smartphones in general and social media in particular tend to impact us in terms of "distorting" our view of the world.

The Effects Are Not Just Physiological or Psychological

Excessive use of smartphones and social media may have significant physiological and psychological consequences such as sleep disturbance, anxiety, stress, lower self-esteem, ADHD symptoms, decreased self-confidence, increasingly reactive behavior and so on. There are, however, other types of issues connected with extensive use of smartphones and social media that are just as worrying—issues that can be classified as cognitive or social misreading.

We made the case in Chapter 2 that humans are social beings by evolutionary design and that a number of social skills are in fact wired into us from birth. These social patterns are so important that the body has developed specific hormones and neurotransmitters to support functions like grouping, bonding, trust, love, rearing, caring and empathy.

What you will see in the following pages is that the way social media organizes and exploits social patterns, such as grouping and bonding tendencies, may lead to diminished impulse control, decision-making fatigue, diminishing of empathy, increased feeling of loneliness and inadequacy, distortion of reality and an increase in antisocial traits.

Does that sound scary? It should because it is. But remember that these effects do not hit everyone in the same way, nor indeed hit everyone at all. But as was the case with the physiological and psychological effects, there is a mounting body of evidence that many users do, in fact, experience some or all of these surely unintended side effects.

Echo Chambers and Confirmation Bias

We humans like (and actually need) to socialize with other humans—to share ideas, thoughts, gossip, news and to be part of groups that share a common interest of some sort (ideas, tasks, hobbies, children, child rearing, politics, cars …). There is nothing inherently wrong in that and certainly also nothing wrong in sharing much of this on social media. After all, where else could you as easily find and interact with groups of people interested in Aston Martin cars, sous vide cooking, fly fishing, movies or postmodern literature? As most of us have come to realize, social media can be a splendid way of finding and sharing with people that have the same interest. But what happens when those interests have other groupings with the opposite point of view—like for instance when dealing with subject matters such as politics, immigration, the EU and Brexit, Islam and so on?

Well, what happens is what has become known as the "echo chamber effect" as the result of "confirmation bias"—in essence that a group on social media defending a particular point of view—for instance, the idea that Donald Trump is a great president (or for that matter a terrible one) will exhibit the same pattern: beliefs that are in line with the groups will be amplified and reinforced by the group, while beliefs and facts that are in opposition to the group's leaning will be rejected.

Over time this echo chamber effect leads to ever-increasing social or political polarization—and pretty soon you get to the point where there is no middle ground—you are either with the consensus of the group or you are not part of the group.

Next what typically happens is cherry-picking of facts and opinions. Media and articles that agree with the point of view of the group are shared. Media and articles that have opposing views are ridiculed or accused of being "fake news." Interestingly, many of these groups are not overly concerned with the pedigree of the "facts" reported—the reinforcement of the overall position of the group is often seen as more important than the credibility of the fact, media or article linked to.

For members of these groups, the next step is confirmation bias, which is the tendency to search for, interpret, favor, and recall information in a way that confirms one's preexisting beliefs or hypotheses. Some of these groups have hundreds or even thousands of participants. As you can imagine, it soon gets almost impossible for any single individual to stand up to the roar of the crowd.

The echo chamber effects amplify the group's belief; the tendency towards confirmation bias ensures that each new piece of information added to the group points in the same direction and any dissenting voice is promptly shouted down with abuse and disparaging remarks. The effects of this are extremely polarizing, not least because the confirmation bias fertilizes and waters the seeds of extremism by reinforcing the views that define a given group most vividly against opposing viewpoints.

For example, a group discussing politics and finding Trump to be a good president will be more likely to endorse the point of view that Trump is an outstanding or fantastic president, rather than endorsing the point of view that he is more or less OK but also has shortcomings. Over time, this tendency is inclined to pull the consensus of these groups further and further towards extreme stances.

Because of the inherent confirmation bias and cherry-picking of news and facts, this seems to happen without the participants actually realizing what is going on.

This kind of social grouping around a point of view has also come to be known by the name "social media tribalism" because the behavior exhibited by many (or even most) of these groups strongly resembles the way tribes or clans tend to self-organize (reinforcing consensus and seeing everybody that is not with the tribe as being against the tribe).

One very real problem with all of this relates to how we humans feel a need to belong to groups and social networks (*real* social networks, mind you!). For many, the relationship to and acceptance of the group is more important than the currency the group deals in. So, you end up with people participating in online social groupings where they will defend extreme viewpoints that they don't necessarily hold, for fear of being castigated or even evicted from the group, should they express more moderate sentiments.

Anyone who spends time on social media will have come across groups such as these—groups that spout strongly held beliefs for or against particular points of views, cultures, ideas, political stances and so forth—and if you have tried to interact with these groups you will also quickly come to see that there is no middle ground—no moderate "on one hand but then again on the other hand" stances are possible. You are either with the

group or outside of it and that leaves you open to being brutally criticized and castigated.

There is absolutely nothing new in humans getting
together to form groups that share a common set of ideas
and identify and reinforce members while seeing outsiders
as "hostile"—we humans have been doing this for many
thousands of years, often with disastrous consequences (the
emerging support for Hitler in the Germany of the 1930s
being an example).

And because there is absolutely nothing new in this tendency, it should come as no surprise at all that you can see the
same pattern happening online with social media.

By the way, we are certainly not claiming that
echo-chamber effects and confirmation bias on social
media will lead to a new world war or anything remotely
like that—we are simply pointing out that this mechanism,
which is ingrained in us humans, is divisive, easily leads to
polarization and extremism and all too often sucks people in,
not because they agree with the group's point of view but just
because they want to be part of groups of people.

Some different types of cognitive bias

In broad terms cognitive bias can be described as a
deviation from norm or rationality in judgment, often
with the purpose of allowing positive reinforcement
or self-rationalization. And we've already explained
part of the neural basis for these biases, namely the
different ways that the old brain and the new brain

processes information and spits out more or less intelligent responses. Here are just a few common types of cognitive bias—most of which can easily be observed in discussions on social media.[15]

- **Anchoring**: The tendency to rely too heavily on a single piece of information when making decisions.

- **Identifiable victim effect:** The tendency to respond more strongly to a single identified person at risk than to a large group of people at risk. Incidentally this cognitive bias is the reason that charities soliciting funds for help in the third world always show individuals at risk in their brochures.

- **Framing effect:** Drawing different conclusions from the same information, depending on how that information is presented (remember the example from Kahneman on names and traits in Chapter 2?)

- **Availability cascade:** A self-reinforcing process in which a collective belief gains more and more plausibility through its increasing repetition in public discourse (repeat something long enough and it will become true).

- **Bandwagon effect:** The tendency to do or believe things because many other people do or believe the same. Think of it as a sort of herd behavior.

- **Omission bias:** The tendency to judge harmful actions as worse or less moral than equally harmful omissions (inactions).

- **Bias blind spot:** The tendency to see oneself as less biased than other people.

- **Anthropomorphism:** The tendency to imbue animals or objects with human characteristics.

- **Dunning–Kruger effect:** The tendency for unskilled individuals to overestimate their own ability and the tendency for experts to underestimate their own ability.

- **Continued influence effect:** The tendency to continue to believe previously learned misinformation even after it has been corrected.

- **Gambler's fallacy:** The tendency to think that future probabilities are altered by past events.

- **Hostile attribution bias:** The tendency to interpret others' behaviors as having hostile intent even when the behavior is neutral or benign.

- **Peltzman effect:** The tendency to take greater risks when perceived safety increases.

- **Reactance:** The urge to do the opposite of what someone wants you to do out of a need to resist a perceived attempt to constrain your freedom of choice.

When Confirmation Bias Leads to Cognitive Dissonance

In some cases, the tendency towards confirmation bias in social groups can lead to another phenomenon known as cognitive dissonance. Simply put, cognitive dissonance is what happens when you are confronted with information that is in opposition to the beliefs or ideas you already hold. The idea of cognitive dissonance was first put forth by social psychologist Leon Festinger in 1957[16] and his theory has since been validated and expanded by many others.

In essence, the claim Festinger made was that confrontation with internally conflicting information leads to discomfort and attempts at avoiding situations where these confrontations occur. In other words, if you are a participant in a social media group that expounds a particular point of view—for instance, the idea that vaccines can cause autism—you can end up tending to avoid being confronted with information that debunks that myth.

That's because when confronted with this information you might end up having to choose between "the truth" (that vaccinations do not cause autism, which by the way has long been proven scientifically[17]) and the comfort you find in the current beliefs you hold and the support of these beliefs provided by the group you are a part of.

Believe it or not, many people with demonstrably "wrong beliefs" (the vaccine example is a good one) would rather continue to believe something that is demonstrably wrong than accept the fact that the truth looks different than they believe it does.

Interestingly—going back for a second to our discussion in Chapter 3 about fast versus slow thinking and about how autonomous reflective processes provide much of the reason that addictive design works—a 2009 study into the neuroscience of cognitive dissonance jointly undertaken by Peking University and the University of Michigan[18] used MRI scans to look at electrical activity in the brains of subjects experiencing some degree of cognitive dissonance.

They found that the greater the level of psychological conflict signaled by the older part of the brain known as the anterior cingulate cortex, the greater the magnitude of cognitive dissonance experienced by the person. In other words, beliefs or opinions that you have internalized and relegated to your "autopilot"[19] will manifest as cognitive dissonance when meeting facts that point in a different direction.

In fact, a study undertaken in 2010 by scientists working for UCLA[20] tried to map out the brain's decision-making process whilst study participants tried to reduce cognitive dissonance (tried to realign positions). The results indicated that active reduction of cognitive dissonance was signaled by increased activity in frontal lobes (the newer part) of the brain. Interestingly, the study also found that the neural activities associated with rationalization (that is, the getting rid of cognitive dissonance by "choosing" *not* to believe the new information you have been presented with) occurs in a matter of seconds—and without conscious deliberation.

It would appear that the older part of your brain is the "culprit" here while the newer part of your brain, with its ability to rationally think things through, does not suffer from the same issues with cognitive dissonance. The brain typically also engages in emotional responses while rationalizing. In other words, as soon as your subconscious system decides to discard new information, the rest of the process is autonomous, and you will most likely feel good about rejecting it. That's why it's little wonder we tend to be so ingrained in our beliefs, almost regardless of what new evidence is put in front of us. And as you will recall from our discussion of the Cambridge Analytica scandal this is also the reason that although profiling works well to sell goods and services it does not really do all that great a job in terms of getting people to change deeply held beliefs or values.

The Sharp Decline in Empathy

Some years ago, the University of Michigan published a study that had tracked the level of empathy of some 14 000 students over a period of 30 years.[21] The study showed a sharp decline in how much empathy the students felt for others over that time, with the sharpest drop being reported after 2000. The study found that students have about 40 percent less empathy now than their counterparts did 20 or 30 years before. But what accounts for this trend?

According to paper put out by P.J. Manney, a chairperson at Humanity+, in the *Journal of Evolution and Technology*[22] the decline in empathy may very well be linked to use of social media. Further, Manney believes this is the result of "compassion fatigue," a term coined to describe what happens when users are over-exposed to images and posts designed to make them feel sorry for others. These are posts that may individually be well-meant appeals for charity or sympathy. But when they join an ever-growing torrent of clamoring for sympathy, it leads to compassion fatigue and over time diminishes empathy.

Another explanation can be related to growth of confirmation bias in social media. If you participate in social media groups with strongly held beliefs that their values or ideas are better than those of others, it seems likely that this would make it easier to dehumanize those outside the group and thus diminish empathy for them—and perhaps by inference for others as well.

Whatever the reasons for this development, that there is a clear link between social media usage and diminished empathy can easily be demonstrated. A study published by researchers at the University of North Florida[23] aimed to investigate the relationship between social media use, empathy and narcissism and found that some aspects of Facebook use did indeed lead to a diminished sense of empathy for some users. As in many other studies, however, the researchers were not able to determine the exact causes or causation.

Interestingly, neuroscience has increasingly linked empathy to your ability to practice self-control—and this research also points to the fact that although empathy is malleable it does have a specific biological component. Researchers at MIT have actually been able to show that an area of the (evolutionarily speaking) newer part of your brain known as the "right temporoparietal junction" (the rTPJ) is linked to both empathy and impulse control.[24] Interestingly, quite a few studies have demonstrated that people with larger rTPJs are more likely to behave altruistically. Studies have also shown that if the neurons within your rTPJ are firing well and connect well to other parts of your brain, you tend to show more openness towards others. It has even been shown that stimulating this area with electrical currents improves the ability to see things from someone else's point of view (which is an aspect of showing empathy). Likewise, if you experimentally disable the rTPJ for a period of time, you will find that this changes your ability to reason about morality and intent!

In other words, these studies indicate a link between empathy and self-control (and in fact it is well known that people who exhibit dark traits like sadism or sociopathy tend to have both low empathy and low self-control). Or as the header of an article in *The Atlantic* about this phenomenon suggested: "Self-control is just empathy with your future self. The same part of the brain that allows us to step into the shoes of others also helps us restrain ourselves."[25]

What we can conclude for the purposes of this book, is that there are some indications of linkage between extensive use of social media and a diminution of empathy. However, these findings are not definite, and little is really understood about the cause and effect of this phenomenon. Certainly, the body of evidence is not as compelling, nor as complete and persuasive, as for some of the other documented side effects of extensive social media usage.

Still, it is an area worth further study. Much of our ability to function as social creatures is predicated on our ability to understand the situation and circumstances of others. Any external factors altering this ability should be considered carefully. Consider, for a moment, the words of American author and motivational speaker, Stephen R Covey: "Most people do not listen with the intent to understand; they listen with the intent to reply."[26]

It would undoubtedly be a better world if we spent the effort to learn to listen in order to understand.

However, a good reason to spend a little less time on social media and a little more time having fun with the wonderful world of books and fiction was provided by Shira Gabriel and Ariana F. Young[27] in a study undertaken by the University of Buffalo titled "Becoming a Vampire Without Being Bitten: The Narrative Collective-Assimilation Hypothesis." In this study, researchers asked undergraduates to read passages from Stephenie Meyer's vampire series *Twilight* and from J.K. Rowling's *Harry Potter* books, after which they surveyed participants as to how deeply they could empathize with the respective literary characters. What they found was that these readers avidly identified with the wizards and vampires they had read about (and felt they had shared exciting experiences with). "The current research suggests that books give readers more than an opportunity to tune out and submerge themselves in fantasy worlds. Books provide the opportunity for social connection and the blissful calm that comes from becoming a part of something larger than oneself for a precious, fleeting moment," Gabriel and Young write.[28]

The Nigerian writer Ben Okri frames that observation very well in these two quotes:[29]

> Beware of the stories you read or tell. Subtly, at night, beneath the waters of consciousness, they are altering your world.

> Without stories we would go mad. Life would lose its moorings or lose its orientations. Even in silence we are living our stories.

The Changing World of Youngsters

Jean M. Twenge, a professor of psychology at San Diego State University, studies generational differences and believes the use of smartphones and social media plays a large role in this development.

Around 2012, I noticed abrupt shifts in teen behaviors and emotional states. The gentle slopes of the line graphs became steep mountains and sheer cliffs, and many of the distinctive characteristics of the Millennial generation began to disappear. In all my analyses of generational data—some reaching back to the 1930s—I had never seen anything like it.[30] The more I pored over yearly surveys of teen attitudes and behaviors, and the more I talked with young people, the clearer it became that theirs is a generation shaped by the smartphone and by the concomitant rise of social media.[31]

Twenge's research—much of which is reported in her recent book *iGen*[32]—points out that this generation of adolescents are different from previous generations—more troubled in some ways but also more open in others. According to Twenge, this generation enters adolescence later, and for them childhood stretches well into high school. It is a generation that spends less time with their friends in person but more time texting and sharing on social media. They experience unprecedented levels of anxiety, depression, and loneliness—but they also "socialize in completely new ways, reject once sacred social taboos, and want different things from their lives and careers. More than previous generations, they are obsessed with safety, focused on tolerance, and have no patience for inequality."[33]

It is worth noting that not all researchers agree with Twenge's conclusions.[34] In an article in *Psychology Today*, Sarah Rose Cavanagh, a professor at the Assumption College's Laboratory for Cognitive and Affective Science in Massachusetts, accuses Twenge of cherry-picking facts to support her conclusions.

These conclusions should, however, still make us wonder if we're on the verge of a monumental shift in the values and attributes that have woven society together for decades, if not centuries. Have we reached the point where smartphones and social media, for good or bad, have altered the social landscape of our youngsters past the point of no return? What should really give us a reason to press pause is that we've put untested technologies into the hands of an entire generation with no idea of the eventual consequences. And this is by far the biggest social experiment the world has ever undertaken and as of this point in time we have no idea where it will take us.

Or, as a Danish professor in neurobiology, Dr. Albert Gjedde,[35] once told Imran: "Soon, there won't be any control subjects left, even if we wanted to conduct an experiment trying to understand the possible consequences of this massive digital transformation we're all in the midst of."

Cyberbullying

Bullying is nothing new—and it is well understood that the ostracization and social taunting of youngsters can have absolutely terrifying consequences. Youngsters that are bullied are often scarred for life, and for some the relentless taunting of their peers leads not just to low self-esteem but eventually also to depression and even suicide.

Unfortunately, social media has made bullying even easier, and worse, it has facilitated bullying that's kept from the view of parents, friends and teachers who might be able to intervene. The issue of cyberbullying is very well researched and not surprisingly, the victims of cyberbullying suffer exactly the same way the victims of "classical bullying" do. Here are some trends reported by comparing several hundred papers published in peer-reviewed journals:[36]

- Both girls and boys are at risk—adolescent girls appear to have a slightly higher risk of being cyberbullied than adolescent boys.
- Cyberbullying in both victims and perpetrators is related to low self-esteem, suicidal ideation, anger, frustration and a variety of other psychological problems.
- Cyberbullying is often related to issues in the "real world"—including school problems, antisocial behavior, substance abuse and delinquency.
- Traditional bullying and cyberbullying are closely related. Those who are bullied at school tend also to be victims of online bullying.

It is unclear just how prevalent this problem is but some sources, such as the US National Center for Education Statistics,[37] report that somewhere between 6 percent and 11 percent of youngsters are victims of bullying. The numbers appear to have increased from the first survey undertaken in 2009 to the latest, which was completed in 2015. Likewise, a survey undertaken by the US Center for Disease Control in 2015 said that 15 percent of students surveyed reported that they were bullied electronically.

What is clear is that a fairly large percentage of our children are being bullied by their peers in this new virtual reality, where our kids get to play all the parts of *Lord of the Flies* every single day.

We know for a fact that this bullying destroys self-confidence, leads to low self-esteem and can lead to future issues with substance abuse. It is beyond the scope of this book to delve deeply into this area—but every parent with children who are online should be aware of the risk of cyberbullying and develop strategies to make sure their children are not being bullied—and teach their children the importance of not bullying others.

In Conclusion: The Road Ahead Is All About the Choices You Make!

Now might be a good place to take a quick recap of what you have seen so far. We started out with an overview of the tech-tsunami we are being hit with—an industry as large as the economy of Germany or the UK. And it is all based on getting your attention focused on their screen or service in order to resell your attention to advertisers. They in turn will try and sell you products, services and entertainment. So, you've seen how there is an interconnectedness between smartphone manufacturers, social media companies, search companies and the millions of advertisers and the billions of users that all come together to form a gigantic marketplace where all sorts of products are hawked using very sophisticated profiling software.

You have had an overview of how the human brain works and understood that there is a big difference between the sort of intense focus and concentration you use when reading, solving challenging problems and learning new things—compared to the fast moving and less reflective part of your brain that is essentially a thrill seeker, always looking to get rewarded with a dose of dopamine and also easy to engage using triggers that may be below your conscious control most of your waking hours.

We have made the case that humans are inherently (by evolutionary design) social animals geared to work together, build trust and bonds, show empathy and cooperate—and that many of these traits actually make us more vulnerable to the ploys online marketers use to approach us. And we have shown you how the exact same mechanisms that lead to gambling addiction (or any other addiction), namely, the dopamine drizzling promise of "unreliable but exciting rewards" are in fact embedded in the design of notifications, news feeds, posting structures, likes and so on—all in order to promote what in the industry is known as "stickiness"— keeping you on the page for as long as possible and keeping you returning as frequently as possible, in order to be able to make as much as possible, by reselling your attention to advertisers.

Obviously, the manufacturer of your smartphone or tablet, whether Apple, Samsung, Huawei or someone else, has a vested interest in the same structures. The more time you spend using your phone or tablet the better chance that you will upgrade to the next model of the same device.

And we have shown you that Google and Facebook (and many other media) together with their advertisers know much more about you than you might have expected. You have seen how data-driven discovery processes have allowed researchers to build very accurate profiles on individual users of social media based on just a few data points. And, you've been shown how this data is used to orchestrate what is shown to you on the web—what Facebook and Instagram sends to your feed, what Google delivers as search results and which adverts you get to see.

We've also shown you a whole world hiding behind those adverts—a world based on data-driven marketing that includes sophisticated landing pages, customer journeys, remarketing and retargeting of adverts, reactivation of abandoned online shopping carts and much more.

We're not saying this is good or bad (it's both—it makes markets more efficient, which is good for the global economy, but it entails an unreasonable degree of manipulation of what the average online user is presented with, which is not fair). So now you know something about the approaches smartphone manufacturers, search engine companies, social media companies and advertisers use to keep you engaged with their services to optimize their chances of selling you more products, services and entertainment.

Finally, we have shown that the use of addictive design and the overall clash between some of the structures of social media and your own inherently social being can lead to disconcerting side effects if you are a heavy user of smartphones and social media.

Specifically, we have provided you with evidence that these technologies can introduce decision fatigue, can weaken your ability to concentrate and focus, can lead to sleep disturbances, low self-esteem, diminution of empathy, confirmation bias, cognitive dissonance and, in youngsters, open up a very real threat of cyberbullying.

What all of this adds up to is the inescapable conclusion that addictive design as it is used in smartphones and social media does in fact have detrimental effects—and that the use of this type of design is predicated on the idea of usurping your attention via brain hacks that especially target the reactive (older) parts of your brain and makes triggering of reward–stimulation for staying online part of your subconscious processes rather than part of your conscious decision regime.

We would like to emphasize that the point we are trying to make is not that smartphones or social media are to be avoided or are inherently bad products. Not at all. As a matter of fact, both of your authors use smartphones and are quite active on social media. But we believe that the issue of unintended side effects needs to be understood so it becomes an easier task for individuals and for parents to decide how best to take advantage of the benefits offered by this technology without having to pay the potentially associated price in terms of lack of concentration, decision fatigue, sleep disturbances, anxiety, cognitive bias and so forth.

In the foreword to this book we introduced the term "digital pollution" and the DFRAG syndrome associated with it to describe the side effects that occur when humans are exposed to an abundance of addictive design. And while the dangers of digital pollution may not yet be recognized by the general public to the same extent as other unhealthy lifestyle choices, as illustrated in the foregoing chapters you will probably now have come to realize that the research into this area over the last 10 years has in fact been extensive, and there is no doubt that the potential detrimental effects are significant and grave!

Here are some of the most common symptoms of extended exposure to digital pollution, as we see them. We presented the same list in the Introduction—but at that point you might have just shrugged these things off as fanciful notions. By now however, you should have seen that we have offered clear and substantive evidence for every point on the list.

Physiologically

- Sleep disturbances. Poorer sleep quality and less of it.
- "Skin hunger" leading to psychological symptoms by lack of touches or hugs by others.
- Neural rewiring. Changes how your brain works over time; a particular concern for children.
- Increased stress levels. Significant increase in physical stress levels.
- Reduced ability to recover from stress measurable in the body's level of stress hormones.
- Less physical activity due to screen time.
- Less sex and intimate relations.

Psychologically

- Reduced mental agility. Decision fatigue and mental overload.
- Diminished impulse control. Increased level of impulsive behavior.
- Problems making decisions. Increased number of "automated responses."
- Diminished attention span. Problems maintaining focus.
- Increasingly reactive behavior. Less proactive behavior.
- Reduced creativity and imagination.

- Decreased self-confidence. Feeling less in control.
- Lower self-esteem: Makes you feel your life isn't interesting enough.

Socially

- Diminished empathy. Becoming less able to empathize with others.
- Reduced social interaction. Moving from the "real world" into the online sphere.
- Increased polarization. Increased participation in negative "tribal" behavior.
- Increased feelings of loneliness. Fear of being left out.
- Increase in antisocial traits. Diminishing of societal coherence.
- Reality distortion. Cognitive dissonance. Echo-chamber effects.

The point of this book, however, is not to usher in a new age of technological Luddism nor to argue that technology is inherently bad, but rather to make it easier for you and everyone else to make a conscious decision on how you wish to tackle and mitigate these effects, so you can enjoy the benefits of modern technology including smartphones, tablets and social networks without being impacted by the inherent dangers of the impulsive, "subconscious" and even addictive behavior patterns that can be triggered by these addictive designs.

We, the authors of this book, are both strong proponents of using more and more technology to solve the many issues and challenges we face. We believe automation, AI, robotics, big data and so on will lead to better and much longer lives for many more people and may eventually lead to some sort of post-scarcity society.

Even though we are only in the early stages of this journey, it seems clear that the myriad of consequences that come from constant interface with a smartphone or other digital platform—some intentional, others not—pose major public health questions. And the consequences for failing to mitigate technology's negative impact on our individual and collective health are dire. Just consider this: if Socrates, Newton, H.C Andersen or Einstein had smartphones, would they even have been able to find the time they needed to change the world? Or would they just have ended up spending endless hours scrolling through Facebook?

Notes

1. http://www.pewinternet.org/2015/01/15/social-media-and-stress/
2. Ibid.
3. https://bit.ly/2NxRN3t
4. http://psycnet.apa.org/buy/2014-33471-001
5. http://www.bbc.com/future/story/20180104-is-social-media-bad-for -you-the-evidence-and-the-unknowns
6. Ibid.
7. Ibid.
8. https://jamanetwork.com/journals/jama/article-abstract/2687861? utm_source=linkedin_company&utm_medium=social_jama&utm _term=1673284607&utm_content=followers-article_engagement- illustration_medical&utm_campaign=article_alert&linkId= 54347688

9. http://www.mdpi.com/1660-4601/8/9/3528/htm?hc_location=ufi

10. https://www.forbes.com/sites/alicegwalton/2017/06/30/a-run-down
    -of-social-medias-effects-on-our-mental-health/#7c61bfe02e5a

11. Ibid.

12. Kardefelt-Winther_et_al-2017-Addiction (1).pdf https://bit.ly/
    2v0hoKL

13. http://www.slate.com/articles/technology/technology/2017/11/face
    book_was_designed_to_be_addictive_does_that_make_it_evil.html?
    via=gdpr-consent

14. https://www.theguardian.com/technology/2017/dec/11/facebook-for
    mer-executive-ripping-society-apart

15. https://en.wikipedia.org/wiki/List_of_cognitive_biases

16. Festinger, L. (1957). *A Theory of Cognitive Dissonance*. California:
    Stanford University Press.

17. http://citeseerx.ist.psu.edu/viewdoc/download?doi=10.1.1.620
    .7330&rep=rep1&type=pdf

18. https://www.sciencedirect.com/science/article/pii/S1053811910015
    545?via%3Dihub

19. The authors recognize the fact that it is hard to point to an actual
    mechanism that allows storage of beliefs or opinions in the older
    parts of the brain. This is an area that requires more research to
    understand exactly what is going on.

20. https://www.ncbi.nlm.nih.gov/pmc/articles/PMC3150852/

21. https://news.umich.edu/empathy-college-students-don-t-have-as-
    much-as-they-used-to/

22. https://jetpress.org/v19/manney.htm

23. https://file.scirp.org/pdf/SN_2014042316520277.pdf

24. https://www.theatlantic.com/science/archive/2016/12/self-control-is
    -just-empathy-with-a-future-you/509726/

25. https://www.theatlantic.com/science/archive/2016/12/self-control-is
    -just-empathy-with-a-future-you/509726/

26. https://en.wikiquote.org/wiki/Stephen_Covey

27. https://www.jstor.org/stable/25835489?seq=1#page_scan_tab_contents

28. https://www.theguardian.com/books/2011/sep/07/reading-fiction-empathy-study

29. https://www.goodreads.com/author/quotes/31425.Ben_Okri

30. https://www.theatlantic.com/magazine/archive/2017/09/has-the-smartphone-destroyed-a-generation/534198/

31. Ibid.

32. iGen: Why Today's Super-Connected Kids Are Growing Up Less Rebellious, More Tolerant, Less Happy—and Completely Unprepared for Adulthood--and What That Means for the Rest of Us, Simon & Shuster, New York, 2017.

33. https://www.amazon.com/exec/obidos/ISBN=1501151983/theatla05-20/

34. https://www.psychologytoday.com/us/blog/once-more-feeling/2017 08/no-smartphones-are-not-destroying-generation

35. https://in.ku.dk/research/albert-gjedde/

36. https://cyberbullying.org/facts

37. https://nces.ed.gov/programs/crime/surveys.asp

Chapter Seven

Making Changes Is Not Easy!

The brain/mind hacks used in smartphones and social media work mainly by finding the weaknesses in the partnership between the older parts of your brain and the newer, and there are many. And while these hacks may be great for the companies that develop them, we think you should be able to decide how to use smartphones and social media without being digitally manipulated.

Our purpose is not to make anyone stop using smartphones or social media—we think both are useful tools and provide good entertainment. But we want to make it easier for you and your family to break the habits that lead you to spend more time online and less time together than you might actually want to. In essence, we want to make it easier for you to make a conscious choice about how and when you use your phone and when you want to take a break and go offline.

Connectivity is a tremendous and important step forward for the human race. It is surely the biggest sea change since the industrial revolution and maybe even more important than that. We believe it is a force for good—that being connected, being able to share and being able to access much more information than ever before is good. But there is little doubt the massive change being wrought by smartphones, social media and the global connectedness over the last 20 years will leave both winners and losers in its wake. That's why we should be keenly aware of how these technologies interact with our sensorium and with our psyche.

The issues you tend to run into with digital pollution can be grouped into a number of categories:

1. Conditioning. Situations where repeated triggering has conditioned you to exhibit a specific behavior in a given situation.

2. Triggering. Situations where you are responding to specific triggers as they occur and let them lead you astray.

3. Escapism. Situations where you use your smartphone or social media to withdraw from what is around you because you feel bored or uncomfortable in the "real world."

4. Drag-along. Situations where you start out with a specific goal in mind but allow yourself to become sidetracked and end up spending a lot of time on zonking out.

5. Meandering. Situations where engaging with your smart-phone and social networks fills out a period of time when you are waiting for something or overseeing something (e.g. at the playground).

6. Task or pattern based. When you use your smartphone for a specific purpose—e.g. playing games or solving sudoku puzzles before going to sleep.

There are probably many more categories—this list is by no means exhaustive and depending on circumstances and lifestyle your own list could look quite different. On top of that you can easily have day-to-day variations that affect your self-control. Ordinary things like lack of sleep, low blood sugar—even being on a diet or watching sad movies can deplete your mental resistance.[1]

To many of us these habits are deeply ingrained and often cause us to act without much conscious reflection—in part, as you will recall, because many of the triggers that set off a behavior have become subconscious and are running on "autopilot."

So what can you do to break, change or even just become conscious of these habits and their consequences? Success requires a multi-pronged approach and a particular set of tools that, as it turns out, translates easily into other avenues of life.

On the following pages we describe some of these tools—and if you go to our website www.humansbeforetech .com you can find even more tools and ideas. What's more, you can share your experiences with others and you can see what worked for them.

The website is free to use and we can promise you, that it employs absolutely no "brain hacks." ☺

Change Means Doing Things Differently

In essence, we're going to help you rewire your brain so that it reverts to the relatively natural state it was in *before* it was hacked. The challenge in accomplishing this transformation is to "massage" these new habits into the sub- and unconscious parts of your brain. There, they can defend your peace of mind without the need of your constant conscious intervention.

Changing a habit requires the following:

1. Understanding the habit—what it is, what triggers it, and what need it covers.

2. Setting a goal for what you want to replace it with.

3. Being able to identify and counter the habit when it takes place with a relevant and well-defined countermeasure.

4. Endless repetition—exchanging old habits with new habits takes a lot of time and energy because you are in essence reprogramming your brain.

Having done so, you then need to develop a sort of constant vigilance. This allows you to maintain your new and more healthy digital habits. You'll still be living in a digitally polluted world where your time and attention will continue to be a target for billion-dollar companies that will always be looking for ways to get inside your head. But now you'll be better equipped to protect yourself!

Sounds difficult? It is.

Replacing bad habits with good ones takes work. But as it turns out (oh, the irony), the exact same circuit box of micro-rewards, dopamine-fueled expectations, behavioral science and trigger points that smartphones and social media hack for their own purposes can be reverse engineered and used to help protect you against further invasion.

Step 1: Life Stories

Psychologists often use a term called "narrative identity," which is the idea that we humans form our identity by integrating our life experiences into an internalized, evolving story of our self that provides us with a sense of unity and purpose in life. Typically this life narrative or life story has everything you normally associate with a literary bestseller: characters, episodes, imagery, a setting, plots, themes, as well as a beginning, middle (where you are right now) and an end you are moving towards.[2] Most people are not acutely aware of this tendency to frame identity in narrative structures or "life stories" but you can actually use your life stories to help you set goals for yourself, if you want to manage the habits in your life.

We suggest you aim to produce four different life stories that identify what matters most to you and how you want things to be in terms of family life, leisure time, own time and work (FLOW).

Your four life stories can as be long or as short as you please. What is important is that they clearly state what matters to you when you are with your family, at work, with your friends or when spending time on your hobbies or interests. Remember that these stories are not set in stone. You can start out with what you feel now, then revisit and revise later. Your circumstances will also change over time. What is important is that you build a starting point for yourself—something by which you can judge your future performance.

Here is an example—Imran's life stories, as they look today:

Family Time:

My family is a place where I daily witness my kids' fantastic development and feel that others love me and depend on me. It's a place where I, through my deep relationship with my wife, experience the world, learn how to navigate in it, and have an intimate space where experiences of light, love and joy as well as worries and frustrations can be shared and processed in deep thought and talks.

Leisure Time:

Here I am free to nurture friendships that matter to me, free to spend time on things that interest me and free to meet new people. I also use this time to reflect on my career and family situation with some of the closest people who know me best, and who I can spend time with without holding things back.

Own Time:

My highest priority is to make my family feel safe and ensure that my kids grow up in a safe environment. I want to make a global impact using my combined medical and technology skills. Moreover, I want to live a healthy life with a certain focus on what I eat and how much exercise I do.

Work Time:

I work because I want to make a difference and feel that I can use my talents and competencies to solve real problems. I have a clear need for self-development through my job and it is important to me that other people acknowledge my skills.

Obviously, these are just examples—and your own goals and stories may be entirely different.

A good life story sets the scene and is open and honest. When you're writing it, remember that it's for you and not for anyone else. In fact, it's good to be careful about whom you do share it with. But it will help you focus on who you are and what you would like in your life.

If you have a hard time getting started you can try starting out each of your four stories with single sentences that are descriptive of you as a person in a particular zone. For example: "I am the kind of friend that … ", "I am a mother who … " or "I am an individual who wants to … "

The purpose of these stories is to create a kind of reference that you can use to guide your future self in making the right choices when habit calls on you. If you have decided to identify as a patient, loving parent, this decision will sensitize you to digital distractions and perhaps stop you from losing focus when your children need your attention.

Think of it as a positive self-fulfilling prophecy: you live up to the positive stories you've created for yourself. In essence, they become your frame of reference.

Likewise, if your life story makes you a creative, focused and diligent employee, you might find yourself asking how that squares with being constantly distracted by Facebook or LinkedIn notifications. You are almost certain to discover that it doesn't, and this heightened awareness will have you making increasingly conscious choices between honoring your life stories or keeping on allowing yourself to be distracted by digital pollution.

Over time your life stories will become small but very effective mental "slogans" that you will use to counter subconscious and impulsive behavior patterns. But remember this will only work if the stories you create are honest and relevant. You have to express your core values, hopes, wishes and beliefs in a way where they can become part of your everyday life and be reflected in the choices you make every day.

Step 2: Mapping out Your Habits and How You Spend Your Time

If you decide to use the life story approach to help you set goals in terms of family life, leisure time, own time and work you might also want to start thinking about how much of your overall time your digital habits are stealing from each area.

It's simple really: just keep a record or diary of your digital habits. Whether surfing, browsing, checking mail or notifications, just make a quick record of how much time you spent and what "zone" you were in (family, leisure, own, work).

Do this for a few weeks or even days and you will become more conscious of your weaknesses and triggers. You may also want to think a little about how much time you ideally want to be in each of the four zones—to deliver on the goals you have set out with your life stories.

By comparing your notes on habits with your goals you will get a pretty clear picture of where you need to improve. Being able to see the problem is an important first step in being able to solve it.

Step 3: Identify Triggers & Cues

This tactic is a little more complicated. It has to do with mapping the relationship between your current subconscious digital habits (which, more likely than not are more a product of "doing" than of "choosing") and how they are triggered.

In this step we're trying to answer two main questions. First, what are the triggers and cues that compel you to respond to notifications, log onto social media feeds, and other distracting activities? And second, is there a difference between how you get triggered in the different zones? For example, perhaps you're more likely to engage with your phone when you are with your kids rather than on the job.

It's important to make notes of your experiences. Understanding and seeing these patterns are what will eventually allow you to change them.

The table below can help but you can just as easily construct your own list of questions. There are no right or wrong answers here. The point of the exercise is simply for you to develop a budding awareness of how you respond to different triggers and cues in your environment—triggers that you may not actually be consciously aware of in your day-to-day life.

	Family Time	Leisure Time	Own Time	Work Time
	What do you typically do when the phone rings?			
Respond instantly				
Mute it				
Send a text				
Leave it				
It's never turned on or in fly mode				
	What do you typically do when receiving a text?			
Look at it instantly				
Respond instantly				
Wait until I can check it				
Don't receive notifications from others but check them regularly				
It's never turned on or in fly mode				

(continued)

	Family Time	Leisure Time	Own Time	Work Time
	When do you typically check your smartphone without an external trigger?			
Don't know				
Whenever I can				
When I choose to				
	How often do you typically check your smartphone?			
Don't know				
Whenever I can				
When I choose to				
	What typically makes you check your smartphone?			
Don't know				
Specific places, like the bus, the bathroom, when I'm in my sofa etc.				
Specific situations, waiting, commuting etc.				
Specific timings, like before going to bed, when waking up, when a TV-series becomes boring?				
Specific psychological needs, like sadness, loneliness, boredom				
Specific practical needs, like information, GPS				
Specific emotional needs, like social recognition, love, self-confidence				
Specific physical needs, like phantom vibrations, "tech-craving or urge"				
Procrastination, when I don't want to do something else.				
Other things				
	How often are you typically interrupted in what you're doing when using your smartphone?			
Don't know				
Whenever I can				
When I choose to				
Randomly				
	How much of the time do you feel in control over your smartphone?			
Don't know				
Whenever I can				
When I choose to				
Randomly				

These kind of questions and answers can also be applied to your social media usage, email handling, gaming and other digital habits you might find problematic. Remember, it's not the deliberate usage that is the problem, it's the impulsive one that you are not fully aware of.

Learning to be conscious of these triggers is really important. You can be absolutely certain that unless you have a conscious plan to counter the pull of the next trigger it will pull you right back into subconscious reactivity to the delight of your more primitive brain parts, which have no larger agenda than simply wanting to get a little high on dopamine and digital flotsam.

Step 4: Plan Your Countermove and Start Acting

At this point you should have a pretty good idea about how your digital habits work. You understand what triggers them and when they occur, and you have a good idea of what you want to replace them with. A few examples:

- **At the playground.** With the kids in a safe area, you can finally let go of the reins and let them run free a bit, right? But does relaxation turn into disconnection because you get carried away with your device? (It's really easy to let it happen when your kids want you to pay close attention as they repeat the same action endlessly!) **Solution:** Leave your phone in the bag and put up with the boredom. Pretty soon it will become less boring as you start getting more tuned in to your kids again.

- **Notification pull.** As soon as your phone vibrates or blinks you feel an urge to pick it up and check your notifications. Once you have picked it up you often end up surfing for an extended period of time. **Solution:** Turn off all notifications on your phone. This way you actively have to decide to get on Facebook to see if there are any notifications for you. It makes a real difference.

- **Boring meetings.** Perhaps while at work you tend to get bored in meetings and end up fiddling with your phone. **Solution:** Set your phone to flight mode and leave it in your bag when you go to meetings. Force yourself to pay attention. If you need to "fiddle" with something, bring a notepad and pencil.

- **"Quickly" checking mails.** A decision to just quickly check your mail easily ends up as a 45-minute jaunt on the social media newsfeed. **Solution:** Set a timer and give yourself five minutes to check mail. Once the timer beeps get offline again.

- **Sudoku in bed.** In the evening you bring your phone to bed and end up spending way too much time playing sudoku, reading newsfeeds or playing Angry Birds before going to sleep. **Solution:** Buy an old-fashioned alarm clock and charge your smartphone in another room.

- **In the cafe.** Everyone else is just sitting there staring into their smartphones. All in their own little digital bubble. Why not just do the same? **Solution:** Leave your phone at home or leave it in the bag. Try and strike up a real conversation—"gee, everyone is always engaged in their smartphones. I think it takes something away from us. How about you?"

- **In the car.** Getting impatient in slow traffic. Tempted to pick up the phone to just quickly check notifications. Dangerous and all—but you'll be quick. **Solution:** Turn your phone off when you are driving. Even handsfree connections tend to slow down your reaction time.

There are certainly many more scenarios like these—the point is that you need to identify as many of these scenarios as you can and to choose a specific countermeasure in advance. And when the situation occurs—the escapism, the quick check of mail, the boredom in meetings, the sudoku in bed—you are well-equipped with the appropriate counteraction.

Troubleshoot Failure

Tough as it is, we might as well accept that with something as pervasive as digital addiction, failure is inevitable. "What's wrong with this method? It doesn't work!" is probably the first thought that could come to your mind when you fail. And you will fail. Because this is not a battle against an external enemy but a battle against your own brain's default setting. Troubleshooting the reasons for failure will typically point to one or more of these three things (remember good old B.J. Fogg):

- Motivation: You didn't believe it was important enough.

- Ability: It was too hard to do or there was an easier alternative.

- Trigger: Your countermeasure wasn't well-rehearsed enough, or you simply forgot to fire it.

You may find it helpful to think like a software developer and retrace your steps backwards from the point of failure. Calculate backwards from these different reasons of failure, so you keep on exploring in order to understand why you fail, to figure out what to do in order to avoid failing next time. Remember, sometimes the thing you want to accomplish depends on a series of events that has to happen first. So how do you get past these obstacles?

Please note, that this is not a do-or-don't approach, because with such a fragile and inconsistent thing as the human brain in control, the only thing you can do is use a trial-and-error approach, where failure is simply a way of learning how to respond intelligently the next time with carefully planned adjustment to your experienced behavioral shortcomings.

In Summary: It's Not Rocket Science, but It's Not All That Easy Either

The first part of this chapter has given you a set of tools to help get rid of unwanted digital habits. In essence they are simple:

1. Decide what your goal is and how you want to see yourself in terms of family life, leisure time, own time and work.

2. Map out what your habits look like now and understand how they act on you and when they occur. Put
them down in writing. Being able to document it is
important.

3. Identify a specific countermeasure to throw at each of
these unwanted habits. Have it at the forefront of your
consciousness when you're going into a slippery situation.
Put this down in writing as well.

4. When you fail (and you will) regroup, analyze why and
rework your goal, motivation or countermeasure to better
respond to the habit you failed at cracking.

It's not rocket science but as you will soon discover it is
also harder than it looks because changing ingrained habits
means fighting against parts of your psyche that are used to
"owning" that particular habit. When your brain starts connecting the dots, and starts forming new associative patterns,
where the subconscious thought processes learn that the (new)
behavior B is better than the (old) behavior A for clear and
measurable reasons—this is when things really start to change.
An important thing is also to make a small symbolic ritual like
a high-five, a "yes, I did it," which tells your brain that you
succeeded, a bit like ticking off a box.

Remember, appraisal is more effective than criticism in
motivational psychology. Finally, it makes sense to actively
try and develop good habits and routines that allow you to
better control the tendency to freeze or choke in challenging
situations, especially when jumping into more shallow waters
than you're used to.

Teaching Your Children Sensible and Healthy Digital Habits

It's easy for children and adolescents to go completely overboard online—there is an abundance of possibilities; everything from games to movies, YouTube, puzzles, Snapchat, Instagram, and much, much more. Kids like the instant gratification provided by the online environment—skills that would take days, weeks or months to develop in the real world are magically bestowed on the user in minutes or hours of gaming. Where adults have a reasonable chance of changing their habits through understanding of their patterns, children do not.

What can you do as a parent?

- You can remember that kids don't do what you tell them but what they see you do. If you become a more disciplined and controlled user of your smartphone or tablet so will they. Leading by example actually works.

- You can restrict your children's online access—for example, by scheduling it. Many families find that providing somewhere between 60 and 90 minutes of online time at the end of the day after homework is done seems to work well.

- You can do things together with them that are fun—for instance (banal as it sounds) instead of letting them play online games all the time, try playing a board game together. You will quickly come to see that everyone can have good fun and togetherness out of this.

- You can talk with them about how, in order to become really, really good at something, you need to be able to

defer gratification and put in a consistent effort now
that will eventually pay off—but part of developing that
discipline also entails not letting yourself continuously get
absorbed in being online.

- You can make sure their smartphone or tablet is set up to
offer the least possible amount of distraction. Make sure all
notifications are turned off for all apps and that the phone
doesn't blink, vibrate, or in any other way try to call their
attention.

- You can restrict the number and kind of apps on their
phone or tablet—look through what your kids have on
their phone and discuss with them what should be there
or what shouldn't be there. Less choice means easier
management.

- You can lead them through more useful online pursuits
than just zonking out on Snapchat. Many parents have
had success with getting their kids interested in offerings
such as Khan Academy (free online courses for kids) or
BBC Quiz or BBC bitesize (also free learning).

- Get them engaged in sports or social activities with other
kids—football, chess club, role playing, drama, fly fishing,
drawing, fencing, hiking, gardening—any and all activities that your children share with others provide a good
counter to spending too much time online.

Remember, your kids are looking for your encouragement
and support, and not least, looking for you to show the way
and lead by example.

The Underlying Psychological Principles

When you try to alter or reprogram your digital habits in essence you are trying to reframe a number of underlying psychological mechanisms. Being able to do so requires stamina, discipline and willpower. So how do you stock up on these nice-to-have commodities?

In the following we present some insights and models that can help you get better at pretty much anything—and that also include a number of ideas for how to build more stamina when entering into battle with habits you want to change.

Building Self-Efficacy

Self-efficacy can be defined as your belief in your own innate ability to achieve your goals—a belief that is to a wide extent predicated on experience and on personal insights.

The term "self-efficacy" was coined by renowned Stanford psychologist Albert Bandura (ranked as the fourth most cited psychologist of all time after Skinner, Freud and Piaget) and he defines the notion as "how well one can execute courses of action required to deal with prospective situations."[3]

So, what's the big deal about self-efficacy? Well, it appears to be involved in everything from psychological day-to-day mental states to behavior to motivation plus things such as whether you feel like you're in control in your own life or not.

People with a strong sense of self-efficacy have been shown to:[4,5]

- View challenging problems as tasks to be mastered.

- Develop deeper interest in the activities in which they participate.

- Form a stronger sense of commitment to their interests and activities.

- Recover quickly from setbacks and disappointments.

While people with a lower sense of self-efficacy on the contrary have been shown to:

- Avoid challenging tasks.

- Believe that difficult tasks and situations are beyond their capabilities.

- Focus on personal failings and negative outcomes.

- Quickly lose confidence in personal abilities.

Consequences like these clearly show how important building self-efficacy is. Maybe the biggest interest with Bandura's work arises from the fact that he describes how you can actually develop this crucial skill. More precisely he points to four major sources of self-efficacy:

1. Master the experience.   The most effective way of developing a strong sense of efficacy is through mastery of experiences. Performing a task successfully strengthens your sense of self-efficacy. However, failing to adequately deal with a task or challenge can undermine and weaken self-efficacy.

2. Use social modeling.   Witnessing other people successfully completing a task is another important source of self-efficacy.

Seeing people similar to oneself succeed raises your own beliefs that you too possess the capabilities to succeed.

3. Use social persuasion. Tell other people what you are doing and why. Getting verbal encouragement from others helps you overcome self-doubt and makes you better at focusing on giving your best effort to the task at hand.

4. Recognize your own psychological responses. Your own responses and emotional reactions to situations also play an important role in self-efficacy. Moods, emotional states, physical reactions, and stress levels can all impact how you feel about your personal abilities in a particular situation.

However, Bandura also notes, "It is not the sheer intensity of emotional and physical reactions that is important but rather how they are perceived and interpreted." By learning how to minimize stress and elevate mood when facing difficult or challenging tasks, people can improve their sense of self-efficacy.

So, all in all, the key messages regarding self-efficacy should be that in order to have a life with all its potential benefits, it makes sense to create life conditions that are challenging, but still leave you with the power to overcome them, so that you can grow through successful experiences. Also, it seems wise to surround yourself with people that are a reflection of yourself, and who you receive constructive and useful feedback from, which you can use in your constant personal self-development.

Entering the Zone—Learning to Focus

What does it actually take for us to be happy? That's a question, which in large part has formed the Hungarian-American psychologist Mihály Csíkszentmihályi's[6] (*Chick-sent-mi-high*) career, and which, through his research, he provides an interesting answer to. After interviewing thousands of people from all walks of life and drawing from Buddhist and Taoist philosophy and techniques for self-mastery, Csíkszentmihályi's research has led him to conclude that happiness is an internal state of being and does not, as most people think, come from external circumstances.

In his popular book *Flow: The Psychology of Optimal Experience*,[7] he proposes that a person can make himself happy or miserable simply by changing the contents of his consciousness, regardless of what is actually happening "outside" —or, as he put it: "The best moments in our lives are not the passive, receptive, relaxing times … The best moments usually occur if a person's body or mind is stretched to its limits in a voluntary effort to accomplish something difficult and worthwhile."[8]

Mihaly Csikszentmihalyi sees this state of consciousness as arising out of situations where you are completely and fully absorbed in an activity, especially an activity which involves use of your creative skills. During this "optimal experience" people feel "strong, alert, in effortless control, unselfconscious, and at the peak of their abilities."[9] In the footsteps of Maslow, Csikszentmihalyi also insists that happiness does not simply happen. It must be prepared for and cultivated by each person, by setting challenges that are neither too demanding nor too simple for one's abilities.[10]

Does striving to attain this level of focus and presence in your life make a difference? The answer is unequivocally yes. Extensive research has shown that being able to master this state of focus and staying "in the zone" for extended periods of time delivers positive affect,[11] life satisfaction,[12] inner motivation and self-directed learning[13] as well as high performance in sports, learning, teaching, scientific and artistic creativity.[14]

In an interview in Wired Magazine,[15] Csíkszentmihályi describes this focus as "being completely involved in an activity for its own sake. The ego falls away. Time flies. Every action, movement and thought follows inevitably from the previous one, like playing jazz. Your whole being is involved, and you're using your skills to the utmost." It is also known as being "in the zone" and has been studied in many disciplines such as sports,[16] music,[17] education,[18] and at workplaces.[19]

Anyone familiar with eastern religion or philosophy will no doubt recognize the similarity of this idea to the ancient concepts of the "action of inaction" in Buddhism or "doing without doing" (wu wei) in Taoism. Also, Hindu texts on Advaita philosophy, such as the Ashtavakra Gita and the Yoga of Knowledge such as Bhagavad-Gita refer to a similar state.

And Buddha, we may observe, is never depicted holding a smartphone.

But thinking more deeply about it, the focus and concentration described by Csíkszentmihályi are actually the opposite of having a distracted mind or brain overload—and helping people achieve this state of mind was therefore a natural part of the model, yes, it might even be a part of the cure for digital pollution. Because if you can achieve the ability to change your mental state, then you become less distractible.

As you will recall from the early chapters of this book, we provided you with an overview of how digital pollution and poor digital habits can prevent you from being able to stay focused and concentrated for long periods of time—and how this, taken to its logical extreme, can prevent our children and the generations to come from developing the focus needed to become world class pianists, composers, brain surgeons, astronauts, fighter pilots, painters, software developers, conductors, film makers or even just competent parents, friends and lovers.

In a sense, Csíkszentmihályi's ideas are the antidote to this tendency—because they show us the promise and joy of challenging yourself at tasks that require every ounce of consciousness and control you have.

Deliberate Practice

"It takes 10 000 hours to become an expert in anything." You might have heard that statement before. It was made popular by the well known US author Malcolm Gladwell who, in his book *Outliers*,[20] cited 10 000 hours as the "magic number" of practice time required to achieve true mastery in a given domain. He gave examples of people like Bill Gates and the Beatles, who spent large amounts of time honing their craft before achieving the great successes we know them for.

The only problem with that version is that it was only halfway correct.[21]

The idea of the 10 000 hours originates from two studies carried out in 1993 by the Swedish psychologist Anders Ericsson.[22] He was trying to look deeper into what factors actually determined the level of skills in top violinists. He divided the violinists into three groups based on their level assessed by external music professors, and then conducted interviews with each violinist to determine the reasons for the differences he found between the groups.

The first and obvious part of the explanation was simple. It turned out that the most skilled violinists had in common that they spent more time practicing. The two best groups spent 3.5 hours a day, while the third group practiced 1.4 hours a day. In fact, it turned out that the most talented violinists had spent at least 10 000 hours of practice.

And it was this partial conclusion that Gladwell made popular, and which caught on like wildfire—a bit like the eight-second attention span of a goldfish. But Dr. K. Anders Ericsson himself wasn't convinced.[23] He called Gladwell's interpretation "a popularized but simplistic view of our work … which suggests that anyone who has accumulated sufficient number of hours of practice in a given domain will automatically become an expert and a champion."

The real truth behind the theory was found in the second part of the explanation of the expert level among the best violinists. Besides the number of hours, it showed that there was also a difference in *how* they practiced. Actually, it turned out that the best violinists were better at practicing with the specific purpose of pushing their brain pattern to its limits and thereby forcing it to constantly improve. Describing this particular kind of training, Ericsson coined the term "deliberate practice."

In his book *Peak: Secrets from the New Science of Expertise* [24] Ericsson writes, "Imagine what might be possible if we applied the techniques that have proved to be so effective in sports and music and chess to all the different types of learning that people do, from the education of schoolchildren to the training of doctors, engineers, pilots, businesspeople, and workers of every sort. I believe that the dramatic improvements we have seen in those few fields over the past hundred years are achievable in pretty much every field if we apply the lessons that can be learned from studying the principles of effective practice."

The principles he's talking about are these:

- Get motivated.
- Set specific, realistic goals.
- Break out of your comfort zone.
- Be consistent and persistent.
- Seek feedback.
- Take time to recover.

Each principle is elaborated in further detail in his book, but these bullets at least give you an overview of what kind of elements are required in successful behavior changes when trying to learn well-structured disciplines. Obviously, it's far more difficult when navigating in the chaos we call "life."

In Conclusion: It's Simple, but It's Not Easy

By now you should have a very good idea of what causes unwanted digital habits and some strategies for breaking them or turning them into something better. We have shown you how to use narrative identities to create "life stories" that help set goals, how to map and analyze the habits you want to get rid of and how to develop specific countermeasures.

And we have thrown three psychological models into the mix that go beyond your digital habits and deal more with how you see yourself as a person, learning to become a better problem-solver and figuring out how to stay focused on tasks that swallow up all of your wherewithal but keep you happy and feeling good about your life.

It's important to realize that you do not need to be a professional golfer, football player or fighter pilot to get into the zone Csíkszentmihályi describes—anyone can do it simply by focusing on getting really good at something they like doing—and that includes parenting, knitting, reading books, looking after your aquarium or playing role games such as Dungeons and Dragons.

Likewise, you do not need to be a secret ninja or an Oxford don to build self-efficacy—all you have to do is start trusting yourself and believing that you can in fact accomplish what you set out to do—including getting rid of those annoying digital habits you are suffering from today.

And finally, you won't probably be starting a new hobby aiming for 10 000 hours of deliberate practice, but at least now you know what it takes for anyone to succeed in shaping their skills to an expert level.

As earlier stated, www.humansbeforetech.com is a website that we, the authors, have created where you can learn more about the tools and methods we've shown in this chapter. Please drop by and feel free to reach out through the website if you have any questions or suggestions to improvements.

We'd also love you to share your experiences with us, if you choose to go ahead and try to use our behavior design tools. We want to share both the positive and negative experiences on the website as well, to illustrate to you that you are not alone in the struggle of fighting with the man—or the woman—in the mirror.

Notes

1. http://persweb.wabash.edu/facstaff/hortonr/articles%20for %20class/Muraven%20self-regulatoin.pdf

2. Much research has been done on narrative identities and there is an overwhelming body of evidence supporting the theory. For example: McAdams, D. (2001). "The psychology of life stories". *Review of General Psychology.* 5 (2): 100–122. doi:10.1037/1089-2680.5.2.100. Bauer, J.J., McAdam, D.P. & Sakaeda, A.R. (2005). "Interpreting the good life: Growth memories in the lives of mature, happy people". *Journal of Personality and Social Psychology.* 88 (1): 203–217. doi:10.1037/0022-3514.88.1.203. PMID 15631585. King, L. A. & Hicks, J. A. (2007). "Whatever happened to 'what might have been'? Regret, happiness, and maturity". *American Psychologist.* 62: 625–636. doi:10.1037/0003-066x.62.7.625. PMID 17924747. Lodi-Smith, J., Geise, A.C., Roberts, B.W. & Robins, R.W. (2009). "Narrating personality change". *Journal of Personality and Social Psychology.* 96 (3): 679–689. doi:10 .1037/a0014611. PMC 2699753. McLean, K.C. & Fournier, M.A. (2008). "The content and processes of autobiographical reasoning in narrative identity". *Journal of Research in Personality.* 42: 527–545. doi:10.1016/j.jrp.2007.08.003. McLean, K.C., Pasupathi, M. & Pals, J.L. (2007). "Selves creating stories creating

selves: a process model of self development". *Personality and Social Psychological Review.* 11: 262–78. doi:10.1177/1088868307301034. Pals, J.L. (2006). "Narrative identity processing of difficult life experiences: Pathways of personality development and positive self-transformation in adulthood". *Journal of Personality.* 74 (4): 1079–1110. doi:10.1111/j.1467-6494.2006.00403.x. Pasupathi, M. (2001). "The social construction of the personal past and its implications for adult development". *Psychological Bulletin.* 127: 651–672. doi:10.1037/0033-2909.127.5.651. Woike, B. & Polo, M. (2001). "Motive-related memories: content, structure, and affect". *Journal of Personality.* 69(3): 391–415. doi:10.1111/1467-6494.00150. Baumeister, R.F. & Newman, L.S. (1994). "How stories make sense of personal experiences: Motives that shape auto-biographical narratives". *Personality and Social Psychology Bulletin.* 20: 676–690.

3. https://en.wikipedia.org/wiki/Self-efficacy

4. Bandura, A. Exercise of personal agency through the self-efficacy mechanisms. In R. Schwarzer (Ed.), *Self-efficacy: Thought control of action.* Washington, DC: Hemisphere: Taylor & Francis; 1992.

5. Bandura, A. *Self-Efficacy in Changing Societies.* UK: Cambridge University Press; 1995.

6. https://en.wikipedia.org/wiki/Mihaly_Csikszentmihalyi

7. Mihaly Csikszentmihalyi, *Flow,* Imprint: Harper Perennial Modern Classics, Canada, 2008.

8. Mihaly Csikszentmihalyi, *Flow,* Imprint: Harper Perennial Modern Classics, Canada, 2008—page 3.

9. Mihaly Csikszentmihalyi, *Flow,* Imprint: Harper Perennial Modern Classics, Canada, 2008.

10. https://en.wikipedia.org/wiki/Flow_(psychology)

11. Clarke, S. G., & Haworth, J. T. (1994). "Flow" experience in the daily lives of sixth-form college students. *British Journal of Psychology, 85,* 511–523.

12. Schüler, J. (2007). Arousal of flow experience in a learning setting and its effects on exam performance and affect. *Zeitschrift für Pädagogische Psychologie, 21,* 217–227.

13. Hektner, J.M. & Csikszentmihályi, M. (1996). A longitudinal exploration of flow and intrinsic motivation in adolescents. Paper presented at the annual meeting of the American education research association, New York. Alfred Sloan Foundation.

14. Perry, W. (1999). *Forms of Ethical Intellectual Development in the College Years: A Scheme*. San Francisco: Jossey Bass.

15. https://www.wired.com/1996/09/czik/

16. http://www.athleticinsight.com/Vol1Iss3/Empirical_Zone.htm

17. https://doi.org/10.1037/a0018432

18. https://books.google.com/books?id=NCySp2NzAm8C& pg=PA119&lpg=PA119&dq=improvisation+flow+Cs%C3 %ADkszentmih%C3%A1lyi

19. https://www.ncbi.nlm.nih.gov/pubmed/20364915

20. https://en.wikipedia.org/wiki/Outliers_(book)

21. http://www.businessinsider.com/new-study-destroys-malcolm-gladwells-10000-rule-2014-7?r=US&IR=T&IR=T

22. https://graphics8.nytimes.com/images/blogs/freakonomics/pdf/ DeliberatePractice(PsychologicalReview).pdf

23. http://bjsm.bmj.com/content/47/9/533

24. http://nautil.us/issue/35/boundaries/not-all-practice-makes-perfect

EPILOGUE

We set out to write this book because we both felt trapped by smartphones constantly clamoring for our attention and constantly pulling us away from what was happening here and now in the real world. If you're with us this far, we guess you must have felt the same, and like us wanted to understand if this increasing reliance on smartphones and social media really is a good idea.

We have sifted through hundreds of studies, articles and papers to get an overview of what is *really* going on—and hopefully you will agree with us that the case we present is persuasive and compelling: smartphones and social media do indeed interfere with the basic functions of human cognition, and uncontrolled and mainly impulsive use can (and probably will) lead to issues such as stress, sleep disturbance, lack of focus and concentration, issues with bonding and socializing as well as subtly shifting your perception of the world around you (cognitive bias).

If your friends and family ask you what OFFLINE is all about we hope you will share with them some of the insights we have presented in this book. Here is a brief recap:

1. Large tech companies use addictive designs to keep you spending as much time as possible on their platforms and

these designs interfere with a number of basic cognitive functions.

2. The use of "brain hacks" has significant side effects—triggered impulsive behavior while reducing your ability to concentrate, focus and stay on track.

3. Human beings are social animals by evolutionary design and social media does not deliver on "real" grouping, bonding or sharing because these functions are fueled by biological processes that require actual person-to-person interactions.

4. Technoference is at play everywhere—in the playground, around the dinner table, at your local coffee shop and even in traffic. But when we escape into the digital domain instead of interacting directly with kids, family and friends something valuable is lost.

5. The speed of transformation we are witnessing is unparalleled—75 percent of people on the planet are connected and nearly half use social media. We have no idea what the long-term consequences of this shift will be in terms of human social skills, empathy and so on.

As we pointed out in the first chapter of this book, the addictive design mechanisms you see in the digital domain are the result of massive and intense competition over access to an extremely valuable commodity—your attention—and the tools used in this competition have a number of unintended, but nonetheless significant and severe side effects. However, please do remember, we're not saying smartphones and social media are bad—we are simply pointing out that there are potential side effects and that you will get more enjoyment and less complications if you think about how you want to use this technology—if you decide when, how often and how much!

The authors of this book are both proponents of free markets and competition—we believe technological development brings growth and helps eradicate poverty—but we also believe that we need to be careful about how we use technology that interacts with us on very fundamental levels.

In essence we hope to see a shift in the near future—a shift towards a more human-centric technology, that is technology designed to help humans augment and boost our skills, knowledge, competencies and abilities by working with our biology and psychology instead of against it.

To our great satisfaction we have noted, that Apple and Google have already begun implementing more human-friendly default settings for their operating systems, allowing users to become more consciously aware of their digital habits.[1,2] But we still need to see the world's largest social media platform—Facebook—live up to the moral and ethical responsibility that comes with being able[3] to directly affect how more than 2 billion users think and feel.

We need technology that helps us become better humans—not technology that makes us less civilized by destroying our self-control.

Will you help us deliver a message to the tech giants?

In all probability, the leaders of Apple, Facebook, Google, Amazon, Microsoft, Netflix, YouTube, Instagram, Snapchat, Tinder and so on, have all begun to realize that change is coming—that their users want technology that does not stress them out or make them feel miserable.

But you can help encourage them to make these changes faster.

On the next page you can see a letter we've written to five of the most powerful CEOs on the planet, asking them to put more focus into making their products human-centric.

We would be very grateful if you would share this letter with others.

If you go to our website www.humansbeforetech.com you can print out copies as well as share by email or to social media—and you can also sign our petition for these companies to take their civic responsibilities more seriously.

It's time to make a change.

Dr. Imran Rashid & Soren Kenner,
www.humansbeforetech.com
Copenhagen & Cambridge

Dear Tim Cook, Sundar Pichai, Satya Nadella, Mark Zuckerberg and Jeff Bezos.

Thank you for bringing wonderful technology into our world. Technology that helps us learn, find, shop, share and connect with each other. The world is a better place thanks to you—your success has created hundreds of thousands of jobs and given billions of people opportunities and possibilities they did not have before. However, as you are surely aware, the competition for securing customers and users' attention has had unintended side effects such as stress, sleep disturbances, decision fatigue, bonding issues and so forth.

As we humans continue to increase our use of smartphones, tablets and social media, it becomes increasingly important that you help counter these side effects by making your products and services more human-centric. The technologies that will lead us into the coming centuries are a force for good but must be tempered by a greater focus on ensuring that their use is safe and without unintended biological, psychological or social consequences.

We think you should work together to set up a well-funded independent organization tasked with studying the impact of smartphones, tablets, VR, augmentative technologies, social media and so forth on human cognitive function and social coherence—that you should task this organization to publish findings and recommendations for making technology more human- centric—and that you should pledge to take these recommendations seriously and strive to integrate them into future versions of the technology you market.

In doing so, you show support for a new paradigm of human-centric technology, and will make not just us, but literally billions of people more satisfied with being your customers and users.

Sincerely,

Dr. Imran Rashid & Soren Kenner
www.humansbeforetech.com

Notes

1. https://www.bloomberg.com/news/articles/2018-05-31/apple-to-tout-digital-health-ar-features-at-software-conference

2. https://wellbeing.google/

3. https://www.theguardian.com/technology/2014/jun/29/facebook-users-emotions-news-feeds

INDEX